ISO 9000 Implementation
for Small Business

Also available from ASQC Quality Press

ISO 9000: Preparing for Registration
James L. Lamprecht

ISO 9000 and the Service Sector: A Critical Interpretation of the 1994 Revisions
James L. Lamprecht

Eight-Step Process to ISO 9000 Implementation: A Quality Management System Approach
Lawrence A. Wilson

Managing Records for ISO 9000 Compliance
Eugenia K. Brumm

ISO 9000 Audit Questionnaire and Registration Guidelines
Praful (Paul) C. Mehta

The ISO 9000 Auditor's Companion and *The Audit Kit*
Kent A. Keeney

Small Business Success Through TQM: Practical Methods to Improve Your Organization's Performance
Terry Ehresman

To request a complimentary catalog of publications,
call 800-248-1946.

ISO 9000 Implementation for Small Business

James L. Lamprecht

ASQC Quality Press
Milwaukee, Wisconsin

ISO 9000 Implementation for Small Business
James L. Lamprecht

Library of Congress Cataloging-in-Publication Data

Lamprecht, James L., 1947–
    ISO 9000 implementation for small business / James L. Lamprecht.
      p. cm.
    Includes bibliographical references and index.
    ISBN 0-87389-350-6
    1. ISO 9000 Series Standards. 2. Small business—Management.
  I. Title.
TS156.L323 1995
658.5'62—dc20   95-37171
                                                       CIP

10 9 8 7 6 5 4 3 2 1

ISBN 0-87389-350-6

Acquisitions Editor: Susan Westergard
Project Editor: Kelley Cardinal

ASQC Mission: To facilitate continuous improvement and increase customer satisfaction by identifying, communicating, and promoting the use of quality principles, concepts, and technologies; and thereby be recognized throughout the world as the leading authority on, and champion for, quality.

Attention: Schools and Corporations
ASQC Quality Press books, audiotapes, videotapes, and software are available at quantity discounts with bulk purchases for business, educational, or instructional use. For information, please contact ASQC Quality Press at 800-248-1946, or write to ASQC Quality Press, P.O. Box 3005, Milwaukee, WI 53201-3005.

For a free copy of the ASQC Quality Press Publications Catalog, including ASQC membership information, call 800-248-1946.

Printed in the United States of America

 Printed on acid-free recycled paper

 ASQC
Quality Press
611 East Wisconsin Avenue
Milwaukee, Wisconsin 53202

Contents

Preface

As the ISO 9000 series of quality assurance systems begins to find its way down the business hierarchy of the industrial and nonindustrial world, small businesses are discovering that they may no longer be able to ignore the pressures of having to register their company to one of the ISO 9000 standards. One of the difficulties with the ISO 9000 standards is that they were not developed to serve the needs and requirements of small business. Because of this restriction, it has been argued that the implementation cost incurred by small businesses can be prohibitive. I do not share that opinion. I believe that *if* the cost to small business becomes prohibitive, it is not necessarily because of any written requirements in the standards, but rather, because the implementation strategies and documentation requirements suggested by some experts rely too much on implementation models borrowed from large enterprises. These models are naturally burdensome when applied to small businesses. Certainly, there is little doubt that the standard's anachronistic reliance on documentation is not conducive to the everyday needs of small businesses who must rely, for survival, on rapid responses to customer needs. Still, procedures need not be ponderous, forms need not be complicated, and the quality assurance system need not rely on an army of auditors and writers in order to be effective and useful.

My experience with small businesses has shown that they do not usually have a part-time or full-time quality manager. Most of the individuals who suddenly find themselves in charge of ISO 9000 implementation have little or no expertise in the field of quality assurance. This book is written for them. My primary objective is to illustrate how the ISO 9000 standards can be effectively implemented *and maintained* by small businesses without necessarily spending large sums of money and/or having to increase staff.

Because the reader may not be familiar with the quality jargon and the many tools or methods currently available, I have included a few of the more traditional and well-established techniques that *could* be used to not only address many of the requirements stated in the standards, but also help you improve your overall performance as a business. In essence, this book is two books in one. Part I consists of seven chapters that explore the following themes: (a) definition of a small business and differences between small and large businesses (chapter 1); (b) scope of the ISO 9000 series—what it is and what it is not (chapter 2); (c) an analysis of the requirements of ISO 9001 with two examples (written in the format of quality manuals) of how to address these requirements (chapter 3); (d) a review of the interrelationship between various paragraphs (chapter 4); (e) examples of how to design forms and write procedures (chapter 5); (f) a complete set of guidelines to help you design and conduct your internal audits (chapter 6); and (g) concluding remarks regarding how to structure your quality assurance manual and what to expect in terms of registration cost (chapter 7). Numerous examples are found throughout Part I.

Part II consists of 11 chapters written to illustrate how various techniques can be used in conjunction with the standards. The following topics are covered: acceptance sampling (chapter 8), problem definition (chapter 9), flowcharts (chapter 10), gauge repeatability and reproducibility (chapter 11), failure mode and effects analysis (chapter 12), cause-and-effect diagrams (chapter 13), data collection (chapter 14), Pareto diagrams (chapter 15), histograms (chapter 16), statistical process control (chapter 17), and design of experiments (chapter 18). Although the two parts are self-contained, the information found throughout Parts I and II constitutes a whole and is intended to be read together.

The book is not meant to convince skeptics as to whether they should or should not achieve ISO 9000 registration. There are plenty of ISO 9000 preachers in the world who will want to convince you that their approach or method is the only way to correctly proceed. I am not one of them. My intent is to present you with options and guidelines. My basic premise is that you have bought this book because you already are seriously considering obtaining ISO 9000 registration, or one of your customers is strongly suggesting that you obtain registration. I cannot promise you that ISO 9000 registration will improve the overall performance or efficiency of your company (although such claims have been made by many). I can tell you this: Going through the process of ISO 9000 registration and eventually achieving registration will *likely* force you to reflect on the way you currently are doing business. It should also force you to rethink some of your current processes. Naturally, I cannot guarantee that these objectives will always be achieved, because some companies only seek ISO 9000 registration because they are forced to do it. These companies are likely to miss valuable opportunities and will probably view the ISO 9000 registration process as a painful and worthless exercise.

Finally, I should explain that, although I have included several examples of procedures and two complete sets of quality manuals (see chapters 3 through 5), I have not included a detailed and critical analysis for every ISO 9000 paragraph.

The examples provided should be enough for you to use as guidelines to write other procedures and avoid costly or even amusing mistakes. Who would have thought that the ISO 9000 series of standards could lead to amusing anecdotes, yet it has. A couple of weeks before I submitted my last editorial changes to this manuscript, I was told the following amusing and disturbing anecdotes about ISO 9000–registered firms. Although these accounts may appear incredible and certainly ludicrous, they are true.

A client of mine was placing an order to one of its ISO 9002–certified suppliers. When the supplier's salesperson asked my client when he wanted the shipment to be delivered, he simply replied: "Oh, I am not in any hurry, why don't you ship it to me the week of June 26." He never expected the following comment: "I am afraid I can't do that, you must give me a specific date." "Why?" my friend asked. "We are now ISO 9002 registered and we must write on all our purchase orders a specific date," was the reply. My client acquiesced and gave an arbitrary date of June 28. The supplier was happy.

This next story is more unbelievable and demonstrates that ISO 9000 irrationality is truly global. A U.S. subsidiary of a European company (it is perhaps best not to mention the country) had received a batch of parts which were packaged in the wrong boxes. Upon receiving the boxes, the quality manager faxed the European head-quarters to inform them of the mistake. The reply from headquarters read as follows: "We could not have made this error because we are ISO 9001 certified." Amusing as the reply was, it was *not* a joke! It is unfortunately true that certain individuals have a rather peculiar interpretation of the ISO 9000 standards. I would hope that after reading this book you will be able to distinguish between ISO 9000 fairytales and facts.

As with my previous books, I have emphasized the ISO 9001 standard, the most complete of the ISO 9000 series of standards. Companies wishing to achieve ISO 9002 or ISO 9003 registration only need to ignore the appropriate paragraphs as shown in Table 2.1 of chapter 2 (see also the appendix for a review of ISO 9003). This book is not a substitute for the ISO 9000 series; it is meant to be used in conjunction with the series. Consequently, I urge you to purchase the appropriate ISO 9000 documents. At an absolute minimum you will need to purchase *either* the ISO 9001, ISO 9002, or ISO 9003 document. ISO 9000-1 and ISO 9004-1 are also recommended. (Purchasing the complete set of documents may be cheaper.)

May your implementation efforts be a pleasant experience.

Acknowledgments

I wish to thank the reviewers for their valuable and helpful comments, which have helped me correct mistakes and clarify or otherwise improve the overall content. I would also like to extend special appreciation to Mr. Ron Muldoon, senior lead assessor with KPMG Quality Register, and Mr. Renato Ricci (Qualitec) of Sao Paulo, Brazil, for their many comments, corrections, and insightful observations. As always, the constant support of my wife, Shirley, has been an invaluable asset.

James L. Lamprecht
1420 N.W. Gilman Blvd. #2576
Issaquah, WA 98027-7001
Phone: 206-644-9504
Fax: 206-644-9524

Part I

Interpreting and Implementing
the ISO 9000 Series

1   ISO 9000 for Small Businesses

> What astonishes me in the United States is not so
> much the marvelous grandeur of some undertakings as
> the innumerable multitude of small ones.
>   Alexis de Tocqueville, *Democracy in America*

What is a small business and why a book on the ISO 9000 series of
standards for small businesses? The definition of a small business var-
ies from country to country. Some define smallness in terms of revenues, others define it in terms of number of employees. Defining the
size of a business in terms of revenues has its disadvantages, particularly when one attempts to compare small businesses globally. A $25–
$30 million business considered small in the United States may be
considered a medium-size organization in Tunisia or other parts of
the developing or newly industrialized world. Defining the size of a
business in terms of the number of employees is preferable because
the number of employees is an absolute number, which is less likely
to acquire a different meaning from country to country. But even if
we measure the size of a business based on its number of employees,
what number should we select—15, 25, 50, or 100? In Australia a

small business is defined as a business with 10 or less employees. In Spain and other Mediterranean countries, 95 percent of all businesses have between 20 and 50 employees.

Mansel Blackford, in his informative *A History of Small Business in America*, observes that "there exists no agreement on what is meant by 'small'."[1] Indeed, smallness will vary depending on the industry. One source of confusion regarding the number of small businesses

> stems from the failure to distinguish between enter-
> prises (firms, businesses) and establishments (branches,
> places of business). An establishment is defined as any
> single physical location where business is conducted.
> An enterprise is a business organization consisting of
> one or more establishments under the same ownership
> or control. Most small businesses consist of a single
> establishment. However, a large firm may own many
> small establishments; these establishments should not
> be confused with small firms.

The confusion is further exemplified when one begins to peruse U.S. government publications. For example, the U.S. government's Small Business Administration (SBA) in 1988 attempted to classify businesses by number of employees. According to the SBA, businesses are to be classified as follows: under 20 employees, very small; 20–99, small; 100–499, medium size; and over 500, large.[3] Yet, the 1987 census of manufacturers, published by the U.S. Department of Commerce, categorized establishments slightly differently (see Table 1.1).

Table 1.1. Number of manufacturing establishments by number of employees (1987).

Manufacturers (359,000)	1987
Under 20 employees	238,000 (66.29%)
20 to 99	86,000 (23.95%)
100 to 249	22,000 (6.12%)
250 to 999	11,000 (3.06%)
1000 or over	2,000 (0.5%)

Source: U.S. Department of Commerce, *Statistical Abstract of the United States, 1993.* 113th ed. (Washington, D.C.: Government Printing Office, 1993), 742.

Of the more than 13 million businesses operating in the United States as of 1990, 7,145,183 were establishments and 6,242,954 were enterprises.[4] The most recent breakdown of establishments and enterprises by size of firm (1987) clearly indicates the importance of small businesses (see Table 1.2).

Nevertheless, despite the slight inconsistency in categorization, the information presented in Tables 1.1 and 1.2 suggests that, in the United States, the definition of smallness agrees with numbers proposed in other countries. Moreover, a recent survey published by the National Federation of Independent Business (NFIB) reasserts the

Table 1.2. Establishments and enterprises by employment size of firm (1987).

Establishments (1987) Total 4,731,694			Enterprises (1987) Total 3,878,866		
0	332,111	(7.02%)	0	330,815	(8.52%)
1–4	1,907,321	(40.31%)	1–4	1,900,185	(48.98%)
5–9	804,865	(17.01%)	5–9	783,793	(20.20%)
10–19	496,651	(10.49%)	10–19	452,986	(11.67%)
20–49	345,658	(7.30%)	20–49	269,305	(6.94%)
50–99	145,297	(3.07%)	50–99	81,914	(2.4%)
100–499	194,219	(4.10%)	100–499	51,076	(1.32%)
500–999	61,386	(1.29%)	500–999	4,590	(0.11%)
1000–9999	192,717	(4.07%)	1000–9999	3,718	(.09%)
10,000+	251,465	(5.31%)	10,000+	486	(0.01%)
Note: 0 employee means that the owner is the sole employee.	< 50 = 82 percent		Note: 0 employee means that the owner is the sole employee.	<50 = 96+ percent	

Source: The State of Small Business: A Report to the President (Washington, D.C.: Government Printing Office, 1992), Table A 4.

importance of small businesses in the United States. The data, summarized in Figure 1.1, confirm statistics compiled in Tables 1.1 and 1.2. It is interesting to note that of all businesses with less than 20 employees (which comprises 75 percent to 80 percent of *all* businesses), over 50 percent of them have less than four employees and over 70 percent have less than 10 employees! In other words businesses, whether they are enterprises or establishments, are dominated by organizations having less than 10 employees.

Based on the statistics in Figure 1.1, I suggest the following definitions.

- A very small business employs up to approximately 20 people.
- A small business employs up to approximately 75–100 employees.
- Businesses having 100–500 employees would be considered medium-size organizations.
- Large businesses employ anywhere from 500 to 1000 employees.
- Very large organizations employ over 1000 people.

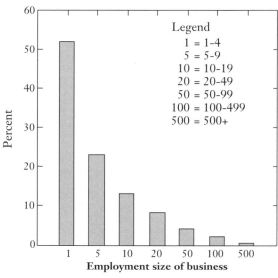

Source: William J. Dennis Jr., *A Small Business Primer* (Washington, D.C.: The NFIB Education Foundation, 1993), 11. Used with permission.

Figure 1.1. Percent breakdown employment by size of business.

This book addresses the needs of very small and small businesses, which comprise the majority of businesses throughout the world.

Was the ISO 9000 Series Designed for Small Businesses?

As one reviews the evolution of the ISO 9000 series and compares its contents to that of other older standards, it is evident that the ISO 9000 series was very much influenced by military quality assurance standards developed in the United States since 1948. Moreover, as one reviews the list of delegates to the various national committees responsible for the development and maintenance of the ISO 9000 series (the Technical Committee 176 or TC/176), it is obvious that small businesses were never represented within these committees. Instead, one realizes that the membership of the various technical committees consists of individuals generally employed by very large organizations, in other words, organizations that represent (in the Unites States and in other countries) *less than 4 percent of all businesses!* As might be expected, these individuals feel comfortable operating within complex quality assurance systems maintained by a staff of quality engineers.

In the United States, many of the companies represented in the top 4 percent (in terms of number of employees), have had a lot of experience dealing with the U.S. Department of Defense (DoD), which requires its suppliers or subcontractors to implement elaborate quality assurance systems managed by a quality assurance director and a supporting staff. Naturally, when the time came to develop the ISO 9000 series of standards, most of these individuals could rely on their experience, and their experience had taught them to work within rather complex and elaborate structures where all activities were performed according to documented procedures and recorded for the benefit of government auditors. Conversations with these individuals invariably reveal that, as far as some of them are concerned, quality assurance activities can only be performed according to one set of activities specified long ago in either one or more military standards, standards published by the American National Standards Institute, standards relating to the nuclear industry, or a convoluted and tedious combination of all three. For example, engineers with years of experience working for organizations that supply the government or provide products that are subject to governmental regulations (environmental, medical, or pharmaceutical, for example) generally assume that the only way to perform design verification and design validation is clearly specified in various government standards, standards relating to the nuclear industry, or standards influenced by earlier government publications. Unfortunately, what is required for major government contracts is not likely to always apply to small businesses.

Small businesses invariably operate in a different world. In the United States, 72 percent of all small businesses operate in retail trade or services, businesses that are not likely to have had much contact with the DoD, the Environmental Protection Agency, or similar state and federal agencies (see last three rows of Table 1.3). Of the 8 or so percent that operate within the manufacturing sector (the percentage has been declining over the past few years), many tend to be either young (less than 10 years old), high-tech companies that have experienced incredible growth over the past six to eight years, or well-established firms that have carved a highly specialized market niche. Some have even managed to double their size every year for six or seven consecutive years! They invariably pride themselves on very fast customer responses, which does not necessarily mean poor product quality. One company that manufactures adapters and connectors for scientific instruments can actually redesign a standard product and/or design a new product and deliver it to the customer within 72 hours! Such incredibly rapid responses, characterized by intense communication and just-in-time design and manufacturing are not only found in the United States. Even a book publisher in Brazil can have a book printed within 30 days of its final editing. Flexibility and rapidity of delivery typifies many of these companies referred to by the business community as *gazelles*. Indeed, among the many characteristics of these small businesses are, as they have been from time, immemorial: product customization, rapid turnaround, and customer satisfaction.

Table 1.3. Number of returns by minor industries (1991).

Minor Industries (enterprises)	Total (1991)	
Total returns of active corporations	3,802,788	
Agriculture, forestry, and fishing	129,886	(3.41%)
Mining	39,199	(1.03%)
Construction	416,987	(10.96%)
Manufacturing	300,122	(7.89%)
Transportation and public utilities	164,980	(4.33%)
Wholesales and retail trade	1,043,534	(27.44%)
Finance, insurance, real estate	617,557	(16.23%)
Services	1,061,657	(27.91%)

Source: Internal Revenue Service, *1991 Statistics of Income* (Washington, D.C.: Government Printing Office, 1994), 21–23.

Types and Characteristics of Small Businesses

Over the past 120 years, one of the immutable characteristics of small businesses is that, in order to avoid direct competition with their larger counterparts, they have tended to rely on specialized short-run production developed to satisfy the unique needs of a particular market niche; versatile use of the most advanced production technology; a flexible production schedule to satisfy a broad range of customer requirements and changing regional markets; and personalized customer contacts.[5] In most cases, the need to develop standardized procedures, favored by larger companies, was certainly not on the agenda of most small businesses; indeed, the need to standardize anything was contradictory to the very existence of many businesspersons operating a small business.

An interesting feature of small businesses is that fewer than one in eight are manufacturers. Often, these small businesses subcontract to larger manufacturers/assemblers (500 or more employees). Generally, the reason for such an association is that the small manufacturer can design and deliver the product in half the time it would take the larger firm.[6]

Nearly 80 percent of small businesses operate in either the construction, finance, retail, or service sectors, which have yet to experience a strong interest in ISO 9000 registration.[7] These statistics are revealing for they closely parallel the percentage breakdown of industries in the United States (see Table 1.3). Indeed, of the 3.8 million enterprises that filed tax returns in 1991, less than 8 percent were in the manufacturing sector.[8] Yet, although the manufacturing sector accounts for a small percentage of all enterprises (7.89 percent), the requirement to achieve ISO 9000 registration is likely to originate from a customer involved in manufacturing. This is to be expected since the ISO 9000 standards, although applicable to all products, are best suited for a manufacturing-type environment.

So why even consider ISO 9000 registration? The truth is that many small businesses are beginning to consider ISO 9000 registration not necessarily because they want to, but because their customers have begun to routinely request that they achieve ISO 9000 registration. This is not to say that many small businesses could not benefit from the discipline required by the ISO 9000 standards. Although some small businesses could be viewed as being inefficient, many are efficient in their own non–ISO 9000 way, and it is no doubt true that, in some cases, the requirement for ISO 9000 registration is correctly perceived as an unnecessary burden.

The events leading a company to consider registration are rather common throughout the world and consist of the following scenario. Company A decides to achieve ISO 9000 registration usually for one of the following reasons: (1) marketing advantage (a competitor recently achieved registration); (2) perceived or real requirement from the European Economic Community (EEC) (called for by some so-called regulated products); or (3) a customer requested certification. As soon as company A achieves ISO 9000 registration, it begins sending letters to all of its suppliers proudly informing them of the fact that it is now registered. Attached to the letter is a questionnaire asking all suppliers the following question (or variations thereof): "Are you currently considering ISO 9000 registration? Yes or no." If you answer no, you must next answer a 10- to 15-page questionnaire that often paraphrases the ISO 9001 standards.

This scenario, repeated numerous times, leads to a cascading effect in which each company that has achieved ISO 9000 registration routinely begins to ask its suppliers to also "look into" ISO 9000 registration. This process is practiced irrespective of the supplier's performance. In other words, suppliers that are fully certified by their customers and are even on the preferred supplier list are automatically being asked the same question about their intent to achieve ISO 9000 registration. Since the cascading process has been in effect for approximately four years in the United States (longer in the United Kingdom), smaller suppliers are now beginning to feel the pressure to achieve ISO 9000 registration.

Why Is the Cascading Process Happening?

There is no reason to require all suppliers to achieve ISO 9000 registration. So why is the phenomenon occurring? In some countries unscrupulous registrars are telling companies they register that all their suppliers must also be registered! Is that necessary? Of course not, but the more companies that are registered, the more business for registrars. In the United Kingdom, where registration to BS 5750 (the United Kingdom's equivalent to the ISO 9000 series) has been aggressively marketed and to some extent imposed on businesses over the past seven years, British companies are already paying as much as 80 million pounds (approximately $140 million in 1994) in annual fees to certification bodies.[9]

In the United States, where the IS0 9000 series has also been aggressively promoted ever since 1990, the movement has experienced several phases. At first, advertising campaigns were warning companies that failure to achieve ISO 9000 registration would lock them out of the European market. ISO 9000 registration was pushed as the passport to Europe that would guarantee worldwide competitiveness. Since 1993, the passport-to-Europe theme is no longer mentioned; advertisers now simply list their ever-expanding course curriculum: ISO 9000 for the defense industry, ISO 9000 for the aerospace industry, the ISO 9000 series and Good Manufacturing

Practices, ISO 9000 and total quality management, how to reengineer your firm using ISO 9000, and so on. The sensationalistic advertisements of earlier years are now reserved for the new QS-9000 and TE-9000 (tooling and equipment) standards promoted by the automotive (Ford, Chrysler, and General Motors) and truck manufacturing industries and the yet-to-be-released (probably in 1996) ISO 14000 series for environmental management.[10]

Faced with the request by their customers to achieve ISO 9000 registration, what can small businesses do? Few options are actually available for small business owners. In many cases, customers either hint or state that they will no longer purchase from a particular supplier, despite an excellent rating, unless ISO 9000 registration is obtained. If the customer is particularly powerful or influential, you will likely be requested to implement your customer's special interpretation of the ISO 9000 series. In the majority of cases, this means that you will be privileged to have to implement what I have referred to as the ISO 9000+ standards. This means that in addition to requirements specified in either ISO 9001, ISO 9002, or ISO 9003, you will also have to implement customer-specific requirements. This is precisely what the QS-9000 automotive standard of Ford, General Motors, and Chrysler have achieved. (Note: In Brazil, the Fiat quality assurance standard imposes similar requirements on many suppliers.)

As more and more suppliers obtain ISO 9000 registration, the pressure on those left unregistered increases. Along with the pressure comes the usual costs associated with achieving registration, and, in recent months, small businesses have begun to express concerns regarding the cost required to implement an ISO 9000 quality assurance system and achieve and maintain registration.

Are Small Businesses Smaller Versions of Large Businesses?
The assumption often made by some consultants and experts is that what is good or works for large businesses is also good and equally valid for small businesses. Nothing is further from the truth. Small businesses are subject to a set of economic problems not shared by larger businesses. Although all businesses are subject to the same laws of economic cycles (upturns and downturns), large companies are

better equipped and more likely to withstand the long periods of economic downturn than small companies. That is why half of small companies are not likely to be in operation five years after their creation. Of course, not being in operation does not necessarily mean that a business has filed for bankruptcy; it might have been sold to a larger organization for a variety of reasons usually associated with some form of success.

Also, small businesses are less likely to have a separate department in charge of the many requirements called for throughout the ISO 9000 series of standards. In many very small and small businesses, the quality assurance department does not exist; one person is in charge of several functions including quality control. This is often due to the fact that the responsibility for quality assurance and quality control is diffused throughout the workforce. In an environment where speed is of the essence, people are allowed and expected to make rapid decisions, and although some records are kept, no procedures are maintained. This leads to one of the main fears regarding ISO 9000 registration. To most business owners, achieving ISO 9000 registration means having to develop a complex set of procedures that will paralyze their current rapid and flexible mode of operation. Of course, if small business owners decide to thoughtlessly mimic the quality assurance system of larger corporations, they will likely run the risk of losing their flexibility and fast response, and eventually their business. But this does not need to happen. I demonstrate in this book how you can implement an effective ISO 9000 quality assurance system designed to suit the needs of most small to medium-size businesses.

Notes

1. M. Blackford, *A History of Small Business in America* (New York: Twayne Publishers, 1991), xi.

2. *The State of Small Business: A Report of the President Transmitted to the Congress 1992* (Washington, D.C.: Government Printing Office, 1992), 20.

3. Small Business Administration Annual Report 1988, p. 19, as quoted in Blackford, *A History of Small Business*, p. xii.

4. This does not include an estimated 4.5 million corporations and 1.7 million partnerships. An establishment is defined as any single physical location where business is conducted. An enterprise consists of one or more establishments under the same ownership.

5. For an excellent account see Blackford, *A History of Small Business*, chapters 2 and 3.

6. S. Solomon, *Small Business USA: The Role of Small Companies in Sparking America's Economic Transformation* (New York: Crown, 1986).

7. For a review of the application of the ISO 9000 series in the service sector, see J. Lamprecht, *ISO 9000 and the Service Sector* (Milwaukee, Wisc.: ASQC Quality Press, 1994). For an excellent account as to why small businesses are not likely to dominate the manufacturing sector see H. Vatter, "The Position of Small Business in the Structure of American Manufacturing, 1870–1970," in *Small Business in American Life*, ed. S. W. Bruchey (New York: Columbia Press, 1980), 142–168.

8. It is interesting to note that the number of manufacturers has decreased approximately 17 percent from 359,000 in 1989 to slightly over 300,000 in 1991.

9. Editorial, *ISO 9000 News* 3, no. 6 (November/December, 1994): 21.

10. The term *environmental management* is odd. Indeed, what needs to be managed is not really the environment, but rather the amount of pollution transferred to the environment by industries. *Pollution management* would be a more accurate phrase, but not as good a euphemism.

2 What Is (and Is Not) the ISO 9000 Series

The ISO 9000 series officially came into existence in 1987 when the following five documents were published by the International Organization for Standardization in Geneva.[1]

ISO 9000-1 (ANSI/ISO/ASQC Q9000-1-1994), *Quality Management and Quality Assurance Standards: Guidelines for Selection and Use*

ISO 9001 (ANSI/ISO/ASQC Q9001-1994), *Quality Systems—Model for Quality Assurance in Design, Development, Production, Installation and Servicing*

ISO 9002 (ANSI/ISO/ASQC Q9002-1994), *Quality Systems—Model for Quality Assurance in Production, Installation and Servicing*

ISO 9003 (ANSI/ISO/ASQC Q9003-1994), *Quality Systems—Model for Quality Assurance in Final Inspection and Test*

ISO 9004-1 (ANSI/ISO/ASQC Q9004-1-1994), *Quality Management and Quality System Elements—Guidelines*

Although not immediately accepted by the world community, the standards' popularity have increased exponentially since 1989.[2] In the United States, where the standards have been adopted as the ANSI/ISO/ASQC Q9000-1–Q9004-1-1994 series, nearly 5500 sites had already achieved registration as of the first quarter of 1995. In the United States, the initial driving force that has led to today's guarded acceptance of the ISO 9000 series has been the fear of being locked out of the European unified economic market. This fear, exaggerated as it may have been, was partly attributed to occasionally inaccurate press coverage.[3] Over the last couple of years, however, the ISO 9000 phenomenon has slowly but surely begun to disassociate itself from the European market connection. Today, companies are asked to achieve ISO 9000 registration irrespective of their exposure to the European market.

Scope of the ISO 9000 Series of Quality Assurance Models

It is important to remember that although the ISO 9000 series was written for *all* industries, its contents and structure favor the manufacturing world. This has led to the greatest source of confusion among those wishing to implement an ISO 9000–type quality assurance system.[4] The difficulty, experienced by many, is in part due to the fact that the standards are not as prescriptive as some users would like them to be. Although the standards do dictate that the user (that is, the supplier) shall have procedures for a variety of processes, not one sentence specifies how anyone should implement a particular clause nor does it state how many procedures need to be written. Indeed, no magic formula exists. This deliberate approach, frustrating to some and infinitely wise to others, is exemplified by the following paragraph of ISO 9001, ISO 9002, and ISO 9003 (all three paragraphs are identical).

> It is intended that these International Standards will be adopted in their present form, but on occasions they may need to be tailored by adding or deleting certain quality system requirements for specific contractual situations.[5]

As for the scope, it is still broad but perhaps not as eloquently stated as the 1987 edition, which reads as follows:

> This Standard specifies quality-system requirements for use *where a supplier* [needs to demonstrate] his *capability to*:

- design and supply conforming product (9001).

- supply conforming product to an established design (9002).

- detect and control the disposition of any product nonconformity during final inspection and test (9003).[6]

Before proceeding any further, it must be emphasized that, as far as the standards are concerned, the term *product* is now defined as "the result of activities or processes." Product includes hardware, software, processed material, and service, or a combination thereof, and shall apply to *intended product* only.[7] Consequently, although the standards have overwhelmingly been implemented by organizations within the manufacturing, processing, and assembly world, they certainly apply, with some interpretation, to other organizations including the service sector.

From a global perspective, the standards represent

- A generic set of quality assurance systems requirements designed as a baseline model for quality assurance, which could be used by any industry that is in the business of providing a product/service

- An organizational structure made up of several interconnected and interrelated components (for example, processes and departments)

- The importance of contractual agreements between two parties: a customer and a supplier (who may be contractually required to achieve ISO 9000 registration)

The Structure of the ISO 9000 Series

The five documents making up the ISO 9000 series are structured as shown in Figure 2.1. The two documents entitled ISO 9000-1 and ISO 9004-1 (formerly ISO 9000 and ISO 9004) are guideline documents and are to be used as reference. *They are not intended as enforceable standards, nor should they be consulted or interpreted as enforceable standards.* I emphasize this point because too many individuals have

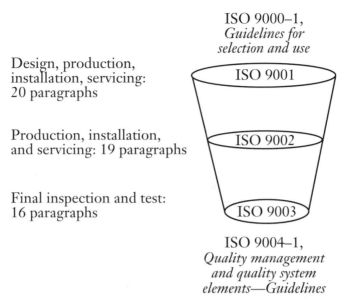

Figure 2.1. Structure of the ISO 9000 series (1994).

made the unfortunate mistake of believing that the ISO 9004-1 document is an enforceable standard.

As for the ISO 9000-1 document, its main objective is to help readers decide which of the three standards (ISO 9001, ISO 9002, or ISO 9003) best suits their needs. The ISO 9000-1 and ISO 9004-1 documents are significantly longer and more informative than the 1987 version. As can be seen from Figure 2.1 and Table 2.1, the core of the ISO 9000 series consists of the three hierarchically nested standards: ISO 9001, ISO 9002, and ISO 9003. By hierarchically nested, I simply mean that as you progress from ISO 9003 to ISO 9002 and ISO 9001, the scope of the quality assurance system is expanded by adding more paragraphs or subparagraphs.

Differences Between ISO 9001, ISO 9002, and ISO 9003

Since servicing has now been added to the ISO 9002 standard, the only difference between ISO 9001 and ISO 9002 is paragraph 4.4, Design Control, which does not apply to ISO 9002. As for the ISO

Table 2.1. List of quality system elements (1994).

Title	Corresponding paragraph (or subsection) numbers in		
	ISO 9001	ISO 9002	ISO 9003
Management responsibility	4.1	4.1	4.1[a]
Quality system	4.2	4.2	4.2[a]
Contract review	4.3	4.3	4.3
Design control	4.4	—	—
Document and data control	4.5	4.5	4.5
Purchasing	4.6	4.6	—
Control of customer-supplied product	4.7	4.7	4.7
Product identification and traceability	4.8	4.8	4.8[a]
Process control	4.9	4.9	—
Inspection and testing	4.10	4.10	4.10[a]
Inspection, measuring and test equipment	4.11	4.11	4.11
Inspection and test status	4.12	4.12	4.12
Control of nonconforming product	4.13	4.13	4.13[a]
Corrective action and preventive action	4.14	4.14	4.14[a]
Handling, storage, packaging, and delivery	4.15	4.15	4.15
Control of quality records	4.16	4.16	4.16[a]
Internal audits	4.17	4.17	4.17[a]
Training	4.18	4.18	4.18[a]
Servicing	4.19	4.19	—
Statistical techniques	4.20	4.20	4.20[a]

[a] means requirements are less stringent than ISO 9001;
— means this element not present.

9003 standard, which used to be significantly shorter than the other two standards, its content has been aligned with the requirements of the other two standards. It is important to note that paragraphs on contract review, control of customer-supplied product, preventive actions, and internal audit have now been added. Also, since the content of all ISO 9003 paragraphs is now very nearly identical to ISO 9001, the ISO 9003 standard is considerably longer than the 1987 version (see the appendix).

Which Standard to Select?
The criteria for selecting the appropriate ISO 9000 model can be found in paragraph 8.2, Selection of Model, of the ISO 9000-1 guidelines.

> a) ISO 9001: for use when conformance to specified requirements is to be assured by the supplier during design, development, production, installation and servicing.

> b) ISO 9002: for use when conformance to specified requirements is to be assured by the supplier during production, installation and servicing.

> c) ISO 9003: for use when conformance to specified requirements is to be assured by the supplier at final inspection and test.[8]

An earlier version of the ISO 9001 document allowed for more flexibility by stating: "during several stages *which may include* design/development . . ." (second sentence of paragraph a). Indeed, installation and servicing may not apply in all cases, and, consequently, should be optional.

Finally, note that, "In third-party certification/registration, the supplier and the certification body should agree on which International Standard will be used as the basis for certification/registration. The selected model should be adequate and not misleading from the point of view of the supplier's customers."[9]

In North America, the ISO 9003 standard seems to be popular in Canada, but not in the United States. In some European countries, specifically France, the ISO 9003 model is viewed as a suitable model for small to medium-size companies. In fact, the use of the ISO 9003 model has nothing to do with the size of a company, but with the type of activity provided. Some warehouses, dealerships, or distribution centers, for example, have successfully applied the ISO 9003 standard. Yet, in most cases, ISO 9002 may be a more appropriate model to adopt.

I do not really know why the ISO 9003 standard is such an unpopular one except to suggest that perhaps the standard, which has fewer clauses than ISO 9001 or ISO 9002, is unjustly perceived as being inferior to ISO 9001 or ISO 9002, or its emphasis on inspection and test is so narrow that most organizations, consultants (including yours truly), and registrars simply recommend ISO 9002 as the appropriate model.

Therefore, with the possible exception of laboratories that may have to comply to the European Norm 45001, *General criteria for the operation of testing laboratories* or to Guide 25, the decision as to which standard to adopt should be rather straightforward: ISO 9001 if design functions are performed; otherwise select ISO 9002 or perhaps ISO 9003.

Common Misconceptions About the ISO 9000 Series

Perhaps one of the most common errors regarding the ISO 9000 series—and this would include professional auditors, consultants, and especially newcomers to the ISO 9000 series—is that users begin to read the standards and start focusing on the documentation requirement of the standards. Although it is true that documentation will be required, do not be intimidated by the task.

As already explained, the second most common mistake is to assume that the quality assurance system must address everything stated in the ISO 9004-1 guidelines. The ISO 9004-1 guidelines should only be used for reference and are *not* enforceable standards. They cannot be used by auditors to audit your organization.

The third universal mistake made by a majority of ISO 9000 implementers is to automatically assume that there is only one way to address each clause. Worse yet, these same individuals are under the incomprehensible impression that the auditors and/or registrars are the official interpreters of the standards and that the only official interpretation can be rendered by a registrar or an auditor working for a registrar. Let us first dismiss these two myths by focusing our attention on the myth of the omnipotent registrar.

The Registrar

Registrars, also known as certifying bodies, are organizations that are in the business of issuing ISO 9000 certificates to businesses. In order to be able to issue ISO 9000 certificates, these organizations must first be issued a license to operate. They can achieve this by ensuring that they operate under the rules and regulations of a set of guidelines contained within a document known as EN 45012, *General criteria for certification bodies operating quality system certification.* Each country operates an accrediting agency (either governmental or private) that is empowered—who empowers these agencies is not always known—to issue a permit to operate as an ISO 9000 registrar for a fixed period of time. Consequently, once an accrediting agency has deemed that an organization satisfies the requirements of EN 45012 and has paid its fees, the organization may then operate as an ISO 9000 registrar.

All registrars are expected to hire certified auditors. This simply means that the auditor has attended a lead assessor course, passed the exam, conducted at least five audits to demonstrate to a certified auditor that he or she has a good understanding of the standards, knows how to audit a quality assurance system, and, most importantly, paid the required fee to one of the auditor certification bodies. Thus the auditor that comes to audit your facility may or may not have any more experience interpreting the standard than you have. Naturally, many auditors will have several years of experience. But, as with all other jobs, the experience simply means that the auditor is likely to have seen more variations and adaptations of the standards. This should mean that the auditor is more flexible and understanding.

Understand that there is no one way to interpret the ISO 9000 standards. In fact there are many ways to interpret them because the nature and extent of a requirement will often depend on the type of industry.

Flexibility and the ISO 9000 Series

Contrary to the general belief that the ISO 9000 standards are rigid and inflexible, the ISO 9000 series actually allows for substantial flexibility as the following quotation will help demonstrate.

> It is emphasized that the quality system requirements specified in this International Standard, ISO 9002 and ISO 9003 *are complementary (not alternative) to the technical (product) specified requirements*. They specify requirements which determine what elements quality systems have to encompass, *but it is not the purpose of these International Standards to enforce uniformity of quality systems*. They are generic and independent of any specific industry or economic sector. *The design and implementation of a quality system will be influenced by the varying needs of an organization*, its particular objectives, the products and services supplied, and the processes and specific practices employed.
>
> It is intended that these International Standards will be adopted in their present form, *but on occasions they may need to be tailored by adding or deleting certain quality-system requirements for specific contractual situations* [Introduction].
>
> For the purposes of this International Standard, the range and detail of the procedures that form part of the quality system shall be dependent upon the complexity of the work, the methods used, and the skills and training needed by personnel involved in carrying out the activity [4.2.2].[10]

As we can see, the ISO 9001 standard (but also ISO 9002 and ISO 9003) allows for adaptability, which is important for small businesses. The quote emphasizes the following concepts.

• The standard is *not* a technical standard for product. Rather it is a model for the management of a quality assurance system. This is important to understand because some people still believe that the ISO 9000 series is a product/technical set of requirements. The ISO 9000 series has nothing to do with product specifications except perhaps to ensure that inspection procedures are in place to verify that product specifications (if such exist) are maintained. How engineering specifications are developed is not addressed specifically by the standards and is only alluded to in a paragraph called Design Control (4.4). The standards are only one of many available systems designed to ensure that a supplier supply conforming products.

• Uniformity of quality systems is not the intent of the standard; variety designed to suit the varying needs of each industry is recognized. Therefore, do not simply copy someone else's system. Design your own to suit your needs. It is much easier and less costly to do so, and results in a more effective quality system.

• The need to tailor the system to particular contractual requirements is also acknowledged. This is very important to recognize because, in some cases, contractual requirements may contradict the intent of the standard. For example, suppose that a customer demands that you use a particular subcontractor that you know is not reliable and is not on your list of approved suppliers. What can you do? Nothing really, except to note on the contract that the customer requested a subcontractor not listed on your approved list. In such a case you would have to tailor your system to suit the customer's request, and this is quite acceptable.

Suppose that you produce a product that is sold for two markets: a highly regulated market (for example, the nuclear industry) and a market utilizing a nonregulated commercial version of the same product. For the regulated product you conduct a formal, detailed, time-consuming (100 or more staff-hours), and, therefore, costly design verification and validation (as specified by paragraphs 4.4.7, Design Verification, and 4.4.8, Design Validation, of ISO 9001). For the commercial product, your customers do not specify in their contract any design verification and validation (and may not even know of their existence). Consequently, you perform a more informal version of design verification and validation, and, in some cases, you may not even perform such activities. What can you do to solve this obvious dilemma? You could tailor your system by issuing a quality plan for commercial products that specifies that design verification and validation, although performed, do not follow the same set of rigorous procedures as for regulated products. In order to do so, however, you would need to demonstrate that this is clearly specified in the contract with your commercial customers. You have another dilemma because your (commercial) customers will never agree to such terms for, although they do not want to pay for the additional engineering cost, they nonetheless expect the same design verification and validation to be performed at no extra cost. What can you do? Perhaps you need to implement a modified, less onerous verification and validation procedure that would allow you to satisfy your customers and the intent of the standard.

• Finally, the range and detail of procedures will also vary according to the complexity of the work, the methods used, and the skills and training of employees. The standard therefore recognizes that the quality assurance system of a manufacturer of paper cups need not resemble the system implemented by an aircraft manufacturer. This should be obvious, but unfortunately is not necessarily recognized by all auditors or first-time readers of the standards. Some auditors audit all facilities as if they were nuclear plants!

How to Read the Standard

Most people, including some consultants and auditors, tend to interpret the standard too rigidly. This can be attributed, in part, to two major factors. Many consultants and so-called experts rely on their previous experience to interpret the standards. This, of course, is logical and to be expected, but if a consultant's previous experience was with a company involved with military, medical, or nuclear standards, that person will naturally tend to interpret the standard and offer recommendations based on that experience. Often these individuals read more into the standards than is stated. Although the ISO 9000 series does find its origins in military standards, one should not confuse the needs and requirements of the military, medical, or nuclear industries with those of other, less regulated or unregulated industries. Others rely on the ISO 9004-1 standard to interpret ISO 9001, ISO 9002, or ISO 9003 and confuse the suggestions offered in the ISO 9004-1 guidelines with the requirements stated in the ISO 9001, ISO 9002, or ISO 9003 standards—requirements that often allow for some latitude in interpretation.

Within the context of ISO 9001, ISO 9002, and ISO 9003 phraseology, there are very distinct grades of requirements. The *shall* sentences are found throughout the document. The majority of ISO paragraphs have a *shall* clause; fortunately (or unfortunately, depending on your point of view), none of the standards specify how you shall do it, only that you must do it! It is therefore up to you to decide how you will implement the requirement (assuming, of course, that you are not currently satisfying it). In a few cases, you may not be required to satisfy a *shall* clause simply because the condition specified in the standard never occurs in your industry. For example, paragraph 4.15.3, Storage, states that you, "shall use designated storage areas or stock rooms to prevent damage or deterioration of product, pending use or delivery." But what if your product is instantly delivered (hence does not need to be stored) and is not subject to damage or deterioration? Examples would include certain chemical products that are delivered via pipelines, or translations (of documents) that are electronically transmitted via telephone lines. Moreover, what about products delivered by architects (drawings) or engineering consulting firms? In such cases, requirements stated in paragraph 4.15.3 may be irrelevant to your business.

Besides the *shall* sentences, the standards include other less restrictive sentences. Examples of sentences allowing a broader interpretation would include the following:

- "Where practicable, the nature of the change shall be identified in the document or the appropriate attachments."(second paragraph of 4.5.3)

- "The type and extent of control exercised by the supplier over subcontractors [will depend] upon the type of product, the impact of subcontracted product on the quality of final product and, where applicable, on the quality audit reports and/or quality records of the previously demonstrated capability and performance of subcontractors;" (paragraph 4.6.2b)

- "Where and to the extent that traceability is a specified requirement, . . ." (second paragraph of 4.8)

- "Documented procedures defining the manner of production, installation and servicing, where the absence of such procedures could adversely affect quality. . ." (paragraph 4.9)

- "The supplier shall ensure that incoming product is not used or processed . . . until it has been inspected or otherwise verified as conforming to specified requirements." (paragraph 4.10.2.1)

- "The inspection and test status of product shall be identified by suitable means." (paragraph 4.12)

- "Where required by the contract, the proposed use or repair of product . . . which does not conform to specified requirements shall be reported for concession to the customer or customer's representative." (paragraph 4.13.2)

- "Corrective or preventive action . . . shall be to a degree appropriate to the magnitude of problems and commensurate with the risks encountered." (paragraph 4.14.1)

- "Where servicing is a specified requirement,. . ." (paragraph 4.19)

As the reader will have noted, several of these sentences allow for additional interpretation. Some sentences clearly state that if a requirement is called for in a contract, then the requirement shall be carried out. This is not the same as saying that the requirement must always be carried out. I have seen auditors misinterpret some of these sentences. For example, a few auditors seem to believe that a supplier will now have to conduct audits of their subcontractors. They cite paragraph 4.6.2b as evidence. But a reading of paragraph 4.6.2b reveals that supplier quality audits are actually optional since records of "previously demonstrated capability and performance" may also be provided. In other words, there are several ways to demonstrate that a supplier is capable of meeting specified requirements. If, for example, receiving inspection records for a particular subcontractor reveal that over the past several months or longer the number of nonconformances was zero or less than or equal to a predefined maximum number, then one can show evidence that the subcontractor is indeed capable, and an audit is certainly not required.

The final responsibility of interpretation is left to the company implementing ISO 9000. The company should not forfeit that right to the registrar or auditor. For example, it is the company's responsibility to determine and clearly define in its quality assurance system to what extent product identification and traceability is required. Similarly, the company must decide whether or not it is practicable to identify changes within documents. The same philosophy would apply to other "where appropriate" or similar paragraphs.

Let us then proceed with a paragraph-by-paragraph description of the ISO 9000 standard. This next chapter provides a summary of the requirements for each of the 20 paragraphs found in ISO 9001 and includes two sample quality manuals that help illustrate how you could address each requirement.

Notes

1. The International Organization for Standardization traces its origins to the International Federation of the National Standardization Association (1926–1939). From 1943 to 1946, the United Nations Standards Coordination Committee (UNSCC) acted as an interim organization. In October 1946, in London, the name International Organization for Standardization (ISO) was finally agreed upon. ISO held its first meeting in June 1947 in Zurich. See H. Coonley, "The International Standards Movement," chap. 5 in *National Standards in a Modern Economy*, ed. D. Reck (New York: Harper & Brothers, 1954).

2. The following seven pages are modified by permission of the publisher from J. Lamprecht, *ISO 9000 and the Service Sector* (Milwaukee, Wisc.: ASQC Quality Press, 1994), 28–31.

3. *Wall Street Journal, Business Week*, and most professional trade journals have carried at least one ISO 9000–related story.

4. *Quality assurance* is defined in ISO 8402 as: "All those planned and systematic actions necessary to provide adequate confidence that a product or service will satisfy given requirements for quality."

5. ISO 9001:1994, Introduction. It is my belief that the 1987 was more elegant and concise.

6. ISO 9001:1987, ISO 9002:1987, and ISO 9003:1987, Scope, emphasis added.

7. ISO 9001:1994, paragraph 3.1, notes 2–4.

8. Quoted from paragraph 8.2.1 of ISO 9000-1:1994.

9. Quoted from paragraph 8.1, General Guidance, of ISO 9000-1: 1994.

10. ISO 9001, *Quality systems—Model for quality assurance in design, development, production, installation and servicing,* 1994, Introduction and paragraph 4.2.2, emphasis added.

3   How to Address the Standard

Most ISO 9000 quality assurance systems consist of a hierarchical documentation structure usually referred to as tiers or levels. The number of tiers will depend on the complexity of the system, but will rarely exceed four. Figure 3.1 illustrates the documentation structure of a typical ISO 9000 quality assurance system (see chapter 7 for more information).

In this chapter, I will present two examples of quality manuals (tier one). Examples of how to write lower tier documents are provided in chapters 4–7. The difficulty with presenting models or examples of quality manuals is that examples cannot be written to suit all industries. As I began to think of some examples to illustrate how to address the requirements of the ISO 9000 standards, I was faced with a dilemma. If I selected an example from a high-tech industry that designs, develops, installs, and occasionally services sophisticated expensive machines used by the aviation industry for riveting wings and fuselages, the reader might think, despite my repeated warnings, that all companies must implement a similar system. If I selected a simpler example, a dry cleaning store for example, the opposite problem could occur—readers might believe that the quality assurance

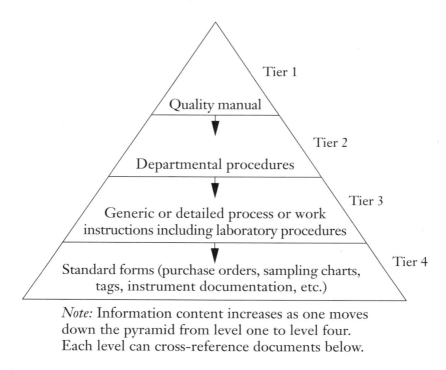

Note: Information content increases as one moves
down the pyramid from level one to level four.
Each level can cross-reference documents below.

Figure 3.1. The pyramid of quality.

system of a dry cleaner would be adequate for their needs. The truth
is that neither system is likely to apply. I solved my dilemma by
selecting two case studies: a well-established low-technology dry
cleaning business and a seven-year-old high-tech company that
develops thousands of standard and highly customized and techno-
logically sophisticated accessories used by scientific laboratories
throughout the world.

The dry cleaning business, ABC Dry Cleaning, employs 12 people. As of 1995, the family-owned business, run by a father-and-son
team, had been operating for 13 years. As a dry cleaning business it
can be considered larger than most. It processes 400–500 shirts a day,
as well as other items such as pants, suits, drapes, and sheets not only
for its own customers, but also for other smaller dry cleaning operations that subcontract their cleaning to ABC Dry Cleaning. ABC Dry

Cleaning is unlikely to ever apply for ISO 9002 registration (the most logical choice for this type of business), nor is it likely that its customers would request such registration. Nevertheless, I have decided to go through the exercise of trying to adapt the ISO 9002 standard to a dry cleaning business (and vice versa) because there are many similar small businesses that may soon be asked by one or more of their customers to implement an ISO 9000–type quality control system.

SciConnect Inc., the high-tech company, employs 35 people and would likely be classified as small or small-to-medium-size in most countries. As of 1995, the company had been in business for eight years. It was started by two engineers, and for the first six years of its existence its revenues grew by nearly 100 percent every year! The 30 percent growth experienced in 1994 was considered slow. It is considering ISO 9001 registration because one of its competitors recently announced that it will seek ISO 9001 registration. The company designs and manufactures a broad variety of connectors, adaptors, tubing, filters, and accessories used with scientific instruments. The engineering staff consists of two engineers (the president often acts as a part-time engineer). Its worldwide client base consists mostly of scientific laboratories or research laboratories and universities.

Both case studies are based on real companies. Since I did not know much about the dry cleaning business, I visited a local one, interviewed the owner, and visited the facilities.

The following text is a side-by-side description of how each business would address ISO 9001 and ISO 9002 implementation and, as is the case with SciConnect, has implemented it. *Note*: The following descriptions could be considered quality manuals; however, please refer to chapter 4 for suggestions on how to control a quality manual.

Case Studies of Quality Manuals (ABC Dry Cleaning and SciConnect Inc.)

ISO 9001 or ISO 9002 Requirements	ABC Dry Cleaning	SciConnect, Inc.
4.1 Management Responsibility	**4.1 Management Responsibility**	**4.1 Management Responsibility**
4.1.1 Quality Policy	**4.1.1 Quality Policy**	**4.1.1 Quality Policy**
This section outlines what you must do.	The owner and staff of ABC Dry Cleaning are committed to maintaining customer satisfaction. This is achieved by ensuring that all items brought to our store for dry cleaning are processed as per customer requirements and are handled throughout all of our processes with the greatest of care.	The mission of SciConnect Inc. is to maintain flexibility and rapid response to our customer needs. This is achieved by ensuring that
1. Management with executive responsibility must define a quality policy, its objectives, and its commitment to quality.		• Whenever possible, we will adapt our products to the varied needs of our customer. To achieve that objective, product reviews, modifications, and delivery shall be completed, when required, within 72 hours of initial request.
2. The policy must be relevant to your goals and expectations and needs of your customers.	Our customer satisfaction is monitored on an ongoing basis by routinely asking all of our customers whether their previous order was handled and processed to their satisfaction.	
3. The policy must be understood, implemented, and maintained at all levels throughout the company.		• Orders are accurately completed and delivered on time.
	Should items be damaged within our facilities, ABC Dry Cleaning will perform all necessary repairs before delivery and at no charge to the customer.	This objective is understood by all employees and is monitored on a regular basis via our internal quality audit process.
4.1.2 Organization	**4.1.2 Organization**	**4.1.2 Organization**
4.1.2.1 Responsibility and Authority	**4.1.2.1 Responsibility and Authority**	**4.1.2.1 Responsibility and Authority**
You must identify and document who has the authority to	All employees of ABC Dry Cleaning have the authority to initiate corrective and preventive actions relating to	All employees of SciConnect Inc. are part owners of the company. They have the authority to initiate corrective and
1. Initiate action to pre-		

ISO 9001 or ISO 9002 Requirements	ABC Dry Cleaning	SciConnect, Inc.
vent the occurrence of any nonconformities relating to the product, process, and quality system. 2. Identify and record any problems relating to the product, process, and quality system. 3. Initiate, recommend, or provide solutions through designated channels. 4. Verify the implementation of solutions. 5. Control further processing, delivery, or installation of nonconforming product until the deficiency or unsatisfactory condition has been corrected.	product or process nonconformities. Recommendations or suggestions can be submitted by all employees for management approval. A review of records relating to product nonconformities is conducted bimonthly (or more frequently if necessary) by the whole staff to determine whether or not changes to the quality system should be implemented (see 4.14). The effectiveness of suggested solutions is monitored during our quarterly internal assessment process (see 4.17), until cause(s) for nonconformities is/are properly identified.	preventive actions relating to product or process nonconformities. Recommendations relating to product improvements are submitted to management and engineering for review and approval. All other recommendations relating to customer complaints, product, or order nonconformities are monitored and managed by the respective quality action team. A report of all corrective actions is submitted to upper management for final review and approval. All corrective and preventive actions are monitored for effectiveness using various process improvement tools and periodic internal quality audits.
4.1.2.2 Resources The paragraph calls for adequate and trained resources for management, performance of work including verification activities such as internal quality audits, for example.	**4.1.2.2 Resources** Most processes such as washing, drying, and pressing require little expertise. Employees working at ABC Dry Cleaning with no previous experience in a particular process receive on-the-job training. The training is conducted by either the owner/manager or an employee with experience in the process.	**4.1.2.2 Resources** SciConnect Inc. ensures that all employees receive adequate training prior to being assigned to a job. All new hires are required to receive from two to four hours of on-the-job training with each of its internal customers. Training lasts approximately 16 to 20 hours, depending on the job or responsibility. All inspectors receive a minimum of two to four

ISO 9001 or ISO 9002 Requirements	ABC Dry Cleaning	SciConnect, Inc.
	All verification and inspection activities are performed by the employee responsible for the work station. Final inspection is conducted by the manager.	hours of on-the-job training. Internal auditors are certified.
4.1.2.3 Management Representative Appoint a manager with executive responsibility to ensure that the appropriate ISO 9000 quality assurance system is implemented and maintained. The manager is expected to report to management about the performance of the quality system.	**4.1.2.3 Management Representative** The owner of ABC Dry Cleaning is responsible for the maintenance of the quality assurance system so as to ensure that the system remains compliant with the requirements of the ISO 9002 standard. Any employee can report to the owner deficiencies in the quality assurance system (see corrective action paragraph 4.14.)	**4.1.2.3 Management Representative** The responsibility to ensure that the quality assurance system complies with the requirements of the ISO 9001 standard and is maintained, effective, and suitable is shared by the president and a delegate. The delegation is rotated to various managers once every year. Any employee can report deficiencies in the quality assurance system to the owner (see corrective action paragraph 4.14.)
4.1.3 Management Review This paragraph is a near duplication of requirements stated in the previous paragraph. Management with executive responsibility is expected to periodically review the effectiveness and suitability of the quality system.	**4.1.3 Management Review** The owner and assistant manager conduct quarterly audits of the quality assurance system to assess the effectiveness and suitability of the quality system (see 4.17). Employee participation and suggestions relating to improvements are continuously sought by management. All sug–gestions are recorded by the owner or the assis-	**4.1.3 Management Review** Management review of SciConnect Inc.'s ISO 9001 quality assurance system is conducted every quarter. The review consists of analyzing audit reports and key performance and process indicators to ensure that the system is effective. Records of these meetings are maintained.

ISO 9001 or ISO 9002 Requirements	ABC Dry Cleaning	SciConnect, Inc.
	tant manager in the Suggestion Notebook.	
4.2 Quality System	**4.2 Quality System**	**4.2 Quality System**
4.2.2 Quality System Procedures	**4.2.2 Quality System Procedures**	**4.2.2 Quality System Procedures**
Documented procedures as required by the ISO standards must be prepared. Moreover, the documented procedures must be effectively implemented.	ABC Dry Cleaning has implemented a quality assurance system that consists of this quality manual and its associated supporting documents and/or operating procedures.	SciConnect Inc.'s quality system consists of this quality manual and the supporting documents and records referenced throughout this manual.
4.2.3 Quality Planning	**4.2.3 Quality Planning**	**4.2.3 Quality Planning**
Supplier should consider • The preparation of quality plans. • The identification of processes, equipment, and resources to achieve the required quality. • Updating quality control techniques and processes. • The identification and preparation of records.	Process equipment consists of 1 Columbia Turbo Dri 103 3 heavy-duty washing machines 1 press for shirts 1 press for blouses 3 steam iron boards With the exception of the Columbia Turbo Dri 103, which is on a routine preventive maintenance schedule, all other equipment is fixed on an as-needed basis. Standards of acceptability are based on visual final inspection (see 4.10.3).	Quality plans are only prepared for Columns (packaging quality) and some Columns accessories. The plans are maintained by the quality control manager (see QC sheets). All nuts are approved via first-article inspection. For parts requiring coating or anodizing, a certificate of analysis or conformance may be required if specified on the purchase order. SciConnect Inc. has three injection mold machines, one tube processor with its own closed-loop self-adjusting system, and several numerically controlled lathes. All of this equipment is under preventive maintenance (see 4.9).

ISO 9001 or ISO 9002 Requirements	ABC Dry Cleaning	SciConnect, Inc.
4.3 Contract Review Management must • Review that requirements are adequately defined and documented. • Resolve differences. • Ensure capability of meeting contract. • Make sure contract amendments are transferred to functions concerned. • Verify that records of review are maintained.	**4.3 Contract Review** Standard orders: For the most part, the contract review consists of counting items brought in by the customer for cleaning. Special requests for starch are also noted on the order. All items are ready for pick-up within 72 hours unless a quicker delivery is requested by the customer. At the discretion of the manager, items submitted before 1:00 P.M. can be promised for next day delivery. Special cleaning requests for difficult stains are reviewed and assessed by the manager or the assistant manager to determine whether or not ABC Dry Cleaning is able to satisfy the requirement. If the task is judged to be difficult to accomplish, the customer is advised of the probability of success/failure and approval or authorization to proceed must first be obtained and noted. All orders are final and generally not subject to any amendment. Should a customer wish to modify an order prior to its execution, however, management will attempt to satisfy the request. See 4.16 for record retention time and storage.	**4.3 Contract Review** SciConnect Inc. has two types of contracts: standard orders and special orders. For standard orders, customers order parts by part numbers as listed in our catalog. Special orders are deviations from our standard product. These requests may consist of customer drawings or verbal or written requests. All requests are reviewed for adequacy and feasibility by engineering and/or R&D. Drawings are reviewed, revised, and/or edited as needed. If required, a prototype is manufactured and submitted to the customer for review and final approval. Once the prototype or drawing is approved, amendments to the contract are appended to the contract by the sales representative, and the order is entered in the company's order entry system. Records of all contract reviews are maintained by sales.

ISO 9001	ABC Dry Cleaning	SciConnect, Inc.
4.4 Design Control	**4.4 Design Control**	**4.4 Design Control**
The standard assumes that requirements are specified. The design function consists of the following eight steps.	This paragraph is not applicable to ABC Dry Cleaning.	**4.4.1 General** The following paragraphs have been approved by the president and constitute the set of procedures applicable to the engineering department. These procedures will be reviewed for update once a year, or more frequently, if necessary.
• Design and development planning		**4.4.2 Design and Development Planning**
• Organizational and technical interfaces		SciConnect Inc. generally does not prepare design plans. In the majority of cases, design suggestions or drawings are submitted by our customers who need customized parts. These drawings are upgraded by our engineers via the review and comment process.
• Design input		
• Design output		
• Design review		
• Design verification		
• Design validation		SciConnect Inc.'s engineers are also involved in research and development activities of new products. These R&D activities are documented in a new project file folder. All projects, whether approved or deactivated (by the president), are maintained within engineering.
• Design changes		

ISO 9001	ABC Dry Cleaning	SciConnect, Inc.
		4.4.3 Organizational and Technical Interfaces All projects, whether generated by a customer request or a new product development, are submitted for review to the appropriate managers. **4.4.4 Design Input** Design input requirements are submitted by the customer and are included in drawings. Incomplete or ambiguous requirements are resolved with the customer, and, once resolved, are entered in the contract. **4.4.5 Design Output** Design output requirements are specified and reviewed by engineering. Key product characteristics are identified on drawings. **4.4.6 Design Review** Design reviews communicated either via phone calls or faxes are an ongoing activity and are invariably completed within 24–48 hours. Records of reviews are maintained by engineering. **4.4.7 Design Verification** Design verification is usually achieved by reviewing and revising

ISO 9001	ABC Dry Cleaning	SciConnect, Inc.
		customer drawings (when available or provided), as required. These verifications are then submitted to the customer for review and final approval.
		Design deviations that do not affect function may, at the discretion of engineering, not require design verifications.
		4.4.8 Design Validation
		Validation is either achieved by the customer who approves a prototype or, via first-article inspection.
		4.4.9 Design Changes
		Changes to designs are reviewed by engineering and updated in the CAD database.

ISO 9001 or ISO 9002 Requirements	ABC Dry Cleaning	SciConnect, Inc.
4.5 Document and Data Control	**4.5 Document and Data Control** The quality assurance manual and all associated documents referenced by the quality manual are under document control as described in this procedure. No particular sets of data collection are required by the customer or are required by the quality assurance system.	**4.5 Document and Data Control** The quality assurance system, as described in this quality manual and its supporting documents, is approved by the president of SciConnect Inc. and is under document control as described in this procedure.
4.5.2 Document and Data Approval and Issue Documents and data must be approved for adequacy by authorized personnel. Documents are available at required locations. Obsolete documents are promptly removed or otherwise assured against unintended use and suitably identified.	**4.5.2 Document and Data Approval and Issue** All documents relating to this quality assurance system are written, modified, and/or approved (that is, signed) by the owner or the assistant manager. The revision status of each document is identified by the date of the last release as well as the previous release date. Master copies of all documents relating to the quality assurance system are maintained in the personal computer and backed-up on disks.	**4.5.2 Document and Data Approval and Issue** All documents relating to this quality assurance system are written, modified, and/or approved (that is, signed) by the appropriate manager or team. The revision status of each document is identified by the date of the last release as well as the previous release date. Master copies of all documents relating to the quality assurance system are maintained in the president's personal computer and backed-up on disk or tapes.
4.5.3 Document and Data Changes Changes to documents and data shall be reviewed and approved by the same functions that	**4.5.3 Document and Data Changes** Copies of operating procedures are distributed in each department. Obsolete documents are removed whenever new	**4.5.3 Document and Data Changes** Copies of operating procedures are available upon request; however, anyone wishing to have access to a procedure

ISO 9001 or ISO 9002 Requirements	ABC Dry Cleaning	SciConnect, Inc.
perform the original review.	revisions are issued (which is rare since procedures are stable). The nature of the change is not identified.	may do so via any of the local personal computers. All computer files have a read only status and can be modified by only a few individuals. Obsolete files are automatically archived whenever new revisions are issued.
		Archived files are retained for the life of the back-up tape, which is about five years. The nature of the change is not identified; however, should a review be required, this can be achieved by simply accessing the archived tape.
4.6 Purchasing	**4.6 Purchasing**	**4.6 Purchasing**
4.6.2 Evaluation of Subcontractors	**4.6.2 Evaluation of Subcontractors**	**4.6.2 Evaluation of Subcontractors**
Evaluate subcontractors for their ability to meet subcontract requirements.	ABC Dry Cleaning purchases two types of products. The first type is products used to package shirts or garments, which do not directly affect the quality of the finish product. These products consist of metal hangers, cardboard adapters for hangers, and plastic bags used to wrap and protect garments. A second type of purchased item consists of various off-the-shelf chemicals used to remove stains. These chemicals require no special specifications and	The evaluation of subcontractors depends on the type of product they manufacture or assemble.
Define the type and extent of control exercised over subcontractors.		For machined parts the evaluation process consists of
Maintain records of acceptable subcontractors.		a) Mailing a self-evaluation questionnaire.
		b) Reviewing the questionnaire by a team to determine capability.
		c) Depending on the result of the review process, visiting the subcontractor for final evaluation.

ISO 9001 or ISO 9002 Requirements	ABC Dry Cleaning	SciConnect, Inc.
	are available from a broad range of suppliers. These goods have been purchased from the same reliable and approved suppliers over the past several years and require no special type of quality control. The criteria for supplier approval are based on the ability of the supplier to regularly supply the products at a competitive price.	For anodized or coated parts, the evaluation process consists of a) Requesting test samples, which are evaluated by the technical staff. b) These samples can be resubmitted until approved. All other suppliers require no evaluation. Records of approved suppliers are maintained by purchasing.
4.6.3 Purchasing Data Purchasing documents shall clearly define the product ordered. Purchasing documents shall be reviewed and approved for adequacy of specified requirements.	**4.6.3 Purchasing Data** Purchase orders always specify the same product and require no special verification since the standard product specifications provided by the suppliers are adequate for our needs.	**4.6.3 Purchasing Data** The verification of purchase orders is performed by the purchasing agent responsible for the order.
4.6.4 Verification of Purchased Product **4.6.4.1 Supplier Verification at Subcontractor's Premises** Language about this clause needs to be included in a quality manual if a supplier proposes to verify purchased product at subcontractor's premises. **4.6.4.2 Customer Verification of Subcontracted Product** This paragraph is written for organizations	**4.6.4 Verification of Purchased Product** Neither ABC Dry Cleaning nor its customers require that supplied products be verified at the subcontractors' premises. Consequently, requirements specified in paragraph 4.6.4.1 and 4.6.4.2 of ISO 9002 do not apply.	**4.6.4 Verification of Purchased Product** Neither SciConnect Inc. nor its suppliers require that supplied products be verified at the subcontractors' premises. Consequently, requirements specified in paragraph 4.6.4.1 and 4.6.4.2 of ISO 9001 are not applicable to SciConnect Inc.

ISO 9001 or ISO 9002 Requirements	ABC Dry Cleaning	SciConnect, Inc.
such as the military, who, for example, reserve the right to verify at the subcontractor's premises that the subcontracted product conforms to specified requirements.		
4.7 Control of Customer-Supplied Product	**4.7 Control of Customer-Supplied Product**	**4.7 Control of Customer-Supplied Product**
This paragraph is written for instances where a customer supplies product to be "incorporated into the supplies or for related activities." In such cases, the supplier shall have documented procedures for the control of verification, storage, and maintenance of customer product.	Since our customers do not provide us with supplies to be incorporated within our processes, this paragraph is not applicable.	SciConnect Inc. does not receive products or components from its customers. Consequently, this requirement is not applicable. Should customers require the incorporation of their product into SciConnect Inc.'s supplies, a procedure shall be implemented to conform to paragraph 4.7 of ISO 9001.
Author's Note: The definition as to what "incorporated into the supplies or for related activities" means varies. If a customer supplies you (the supplier or subcontractor) with components or subassemblies that must then be incorporated into the final (delivered) product, or if the customer provides you with tools, dies, equipment, machinery, etc. to manufacture or assemble a product, you will need to address paragraph 4.7.	*Author's Note:* The opposite argument could be made. This argument would suggest that since the customer provides clothes to the dry cleaner, paragraph 4.7 is certainly applicable. In this case, dry cleaners must carefully control customer-supplied products or they will quickly be out of business. I rely on paragraph 4.8 to take care of the traceability and identification of the customers' clothes. I have therefore interpreted the paragraph to mean that the product supplied by the customer is not incorporated into or with final product; the final product is delivered by the supplier. Since cleaned or dry-cleaned clothes are the final	
The last sentence of the paragraph is important: "Verification by the sup-		

ISO 9001 or ISO 9002 Requirements	ABC Dry Cleaning	SciConnect, Inc.
plier does not absolve the customer of the responsibility to provide acceptable product." In the case of the dry cleaner (next column), an example of a customer-supplied product would be dry cleaning agent, hangers, and so on.	product, I do not consider the clothes to be customer-supplied product in the sense suggested in paragraph 4.7. If you accept that interpretation, then the above statement is correct. If you disagree, then, modify the statement to reflect your actions.	
4.8 Product Identification and Traceability	**4.8 Product Identification and Traceability**	**4.8 Product Identification and Traceability**
Where appropriate, traceability and identification of product shall be maintained and documented from receipt and during all stages of production, delivery, and installation, as required. If traceability is a specified requirement, a procedure defining how items and/or batches are identified will need to be established.	Product identification is not a customer requirement, but is essential to ensure that orders are complete and items are not mismatched prior to final wrapping. This is ensured by assigning each item within a batch of clothes with a unique batch number. That number is used to trace all items prior to final wrapping. Clothes received from other stores are identified with different-colored tags.	Product identification and traceability is required for only one of our hundreds of customers. SciConnect Inc. maintains internal product identification numbers, which allow for traceability by date of assembly, operator, and subcomponents, for its columns and column accessories. Tubing, adapters, pump accessories, valves and other items are identified by a batch number indicating the day of production.
4.9 Process Control	**4.9 Process Control**	**4.9 Process Control**
The supplier shall ensure that processes that directly affect quality are under controlled conditions. Common steps to control the process are	ABC Dry Cleaning does not install or service its product. Its activities are limited to the dry cleaning or washing of clothes, drapes, or sheets. In order to perform these activities,	SciConnect Inc. does not install or service its products. It does provide technical assistance (see 4.19). Manufacturing processes are performed by nu-

ISO 9001 or ISO 9002 Requirements	ABC Dry Cleaning	SciConnect, Inc.
• Documented procedure for production and/or installation and/or servicing • Use of suitable production, and/or installation, and/or servicing equipment and suitable working environment • Compliance with standards/codes, quality plans, and/or documented procedures • Monitoring of process parameters and product characteristics • Approval and maintenance of process equipment • Well-defined criteria for workmanship • Identification and qualification of special processes, equipment, and operators of such processes	ABC Dry Cleaning operates in compliance with all city, county, and federal ordinances that apply to the daily operation (including proper disposal of hazardous chemicals) of a dry cleaning business. Production equipment and working environment are adequate to perform tasks. Due to the nature of the work, ABC Dry Cleaning does not rely on documented operating procedures to define the various dry cleaning or washing operations. When required, these skills are acquired via on-the-job training and are transmitted by employees with the highest seniority or by the owner or assistant manager. With the exception of the dry cleaning equipment, which requires monitoring of the solvent's temperature, none of the machines and processes require any special monitoring beyond those already provided through standard machine settings. Criteria of workmanship, inspecting each item for cleanliness and damage, are assessed by each operator and are verified during final in-	merically controlled injection molds, lathes, or tubing equipment. These machines are programmed by the manufacturing engineer or technician(s) who have the proper technical experience, training, or both. Assembly consists of picking products from stock for assembly packaging. No specific work instructions are required (see training 4.18). All equipment and the work environment at SciConnect Inc. conform to OSHA requirements. Conformance to various American National Standard Institute (ANSI) standards and/or electrical standards or codes are provided by the manufacturer and are filed in the office of the appropriate manager. Chemicals subject to the Environmental Protection Agency (EPA) and the State Washington Department of Ecology regulations are stored and disposed by a government-approved third party. The only key process parameter statistically monitored for process and product capability is the inside diameter for tubing (see 4.20).

ISO 9001 or ISO 9002 Requirements	ABC Dry Cleaning	SciConnect, Inc.
	spection (see paragraph 4.13 and 4.14). The Columbia Turbo Dri 103 is under a routine maintenance schedule. All other machines are fixed by the owner on an as-needed basis. ABC Dry Cleaning does not have any special processes.	Workmanship standards are written on all work orders and are monitored by each operator. Preventive maintenance is performed by the equipment operator. Records of maintenance are kept by the operators. SciConnect Inc. does not have special processes.
4.10 Inspection and Testing **4.10. 1 General** Procedures shall be established to define the following activities. **4.10.2 Receiving Inspection and Testing** Incoming product should not be used or processed until it has been inspected (according to documented procedures) *or otherwise verified as conforming* to specified requirements. The extent of receiving inspection will depend on the control exercised by the subcontractor and evidence of conformance. If incoming product is released for urgent use prior to verification, it shall be positively identified and recorded to al-	**4.10 Inspection and Testing** ABC Dry Cleaning does not perform receiving inspection on incoming products (such as chemicals and solvents) for primarily two reasons: it does not have the competence nor the resources to test product, nor does it find it necessary to evaluate or assess the quality of these off-the-shelf, standard products. Also, suppliers have demonstrated ample control over their processes over the years. Clothes submitted by our customers, however, are subject to 100 percent visual inspection in the customer's presence to identify any damage prior to acceptance of goods. Release of incoming product for urgent production does not apply.	**4.10 Inspection and Testing** **4.10.1 General** Inspection and testing procedures at SciConnect Inc. consist of the following: **4.10.2 Receiving Inspection and Testing** • Subcontracted machined parts are inspected as per MIL-STD-105D acceptance sampling plan. • Off-the-shelf items are verified for part number accuracy and visual inspection. • Chemicals are not inspected. • Some metal stock is dimensionally verified and visually checked for abnormalities. • Stock received for research and develop-

ISO 9001 or ISO 9002 Requirements	ABC Dry Cleaning	SciConnect, Inc.
low for recall in the event of nonconformity.		ment is not subject to receiving inspection.
4.10.3 In-Process Inspection and Testing Inspect and test the product as required by documented procedures or quality plans. Hold product until all tests or inspections have been received and verified.	**4.10.3 In-Process Inspection and Testing** Product is visually inspected by all operators. Defects of unacceptable products are reviewed by the assistant manager and reprocessed if required (see 4.13)	**4.10.3 In-Process Inspection and Testing** • Extrusion lines are under computerized statistical process control • High-pressure items are sampled and tested according to specifications Records of inspection sheets are submitted to quality control.
4.10.4 Final Inspection and Testing Final inspection, conducted according to procedures or defined by the quality plan, shall ensure that the finished product conforms to specified requirements. Product shall not be released until all inspection activities have been satisfactorily completed and the associated document and/or data authorized.	**4.10.4 Final Inspection and Testing** All items are visually inspected for damage and proper matching by the manager or assistant manager prior to final wrapping.	**4.10.4 Final Inspection and Testing** Prior to shipping, all packages and work orders are inspected to ensure that all inspection and/or tests have been performed and all records are completed.
4.10.5 Inspection and Test Records Evidence of the above activities shall be demonstrated via records that clearly indicate whether or not the product has passed an inspection and/or test. If the product fails, paragraph 4.13 applies.	**4.10.5 Inspection and Test Records** The only record of final inspection consists of the original work order (purchase order), which indicates that the job has been satisfactorily completed. The work order can only be attached to the completed order	**4.10.5 Inspection and Test Records** All inspection and test records identifying the person who conducted the test are maintained by quality control.

ISO 9001 or ISO 9002 Requirements	ABC Dry Cleaning	SciConnect, Inc.
The intent of these clauses is to ensure that the supplier conducts the required inspections and/or testing of products from receiving to final inspection. Records identifying the result of inspection or testing must be maintained.	once management accepts the order as satisfactory. Since final inspections can only be performed by the owner or the assistant manager, signature or initials are not recorded except when an order must be reprocessed and requires managerial approval.	
4.11 Control of Inspection, Measuring, and Test Equipment The clause also covers test software and test hardware used for inspection. The paragraph applies for "inspection, measuring and test equipment used by the supplier to demonstrate the conformance of product to the specified requirements." See definition 3.1 note 4 of ISO 9001 or ISO 8402. **4.11.2 Control Procedure** The paragraph includes several requirements. Determine the measurements to be made and the accuracy required. Identify equipment that can affect product quality and calibrate and adjust it at prescribed intervals.	**4.11 Control of Inspection, Measuring, and Test Equipment** Since conformance of product is defined by the subjective evaluation of cleanliness, no customer nor industry specifications currently exist. Consequently, no inspection, measuring, or test equipment is used by ABC Dry Cleaning to demonstrate conformance of product to specified requirements. This is achieved via visual inspection. The performance, or capability, of the dry cleaning machine is maintained by ensuring that its recycled solvents (one for dark colored clothes and one for lighter colored clothes) are replaced once a month. This replacement is automatically monitored and performed by the machine.	**4.11 Control of Inspection, Measuring, and Test Equipment** The only equipment used to test or otherwise inspect a product for customer specification is the pressure analyzers (2). Although these analyzers are certified by the manufacturer to well within SciConnect's requirements, the analyzers are calibrated and verified for accuracy by a third party once a year (June or July). Most instruments, such as micrometers and calipers, for example, are not used to measure key characteristics. These instruments are calibrated (using Mitutoyo™ blocks) and assessed for precision in house. The frequency for all instruments is April, August, and December unless otherwise required. Certified secondary stan-

ISO 9001 or ISO 9002 Requirements	ABC Dry Cleaning	SciConnect, Inc.
Define the calibration process and maintain calibration records. Ensure suitable environmental conditions for calibration. Safeguard equipment via proper handling and storage.		dards are used for all calibration requirements. Procedures follow manufacturer's recommendations. Gauge R&R studies will be conducted periodically—for investigation purposes only and on an as-needed basis—on a random set of instruments to determine if the accuracy has been compromised. A 40 percent R&R will be considered acceptable. Larger percentages will result in the instrument's removal from service. Records of all calibration activities are maintained in a computer database.
4.12 Inspection and Test Status Inspection and test status of product shall be identified by suitable means, which indicate the conformance or nonconformance of product with regard to inspection and test performed.	**4.12 Inspection and Test Status** The only inspections consist of visual inspections conducted during final pressing, ironing, or bagging. All completed orders are identified with a color tag and customer identification number. The owner or assistant manager is responsible for all final releases and authorizes concessions.	**4.12 Inspection and Test Status** The inspection and test status is performed as required by work order instructions and procedures already specified (see 4.10).
4.13 Control of Nonconforming Product	**4.13 Control of Nonconforming Product** Typical nonconformities consist of broken	**4.13 Control of Nonconforming Product**

ISO 9001 or ISO 9002 Requirements	ABC Dry Cleaning	SciConnect, Inc.
	buttons and tears or stains that were not successfully removed. For minor nonconformances, operators are responsible for repair. Tears and/or other damages deemed major are submitted to the assistant manager or the owner for review and disposition. The owner decides on a case-by-case basis what corrective action will be required. Stubborn stains are reviewed by the assistant manager or owner to determine whether or not the item should be reprocessed or accepted as-is (in which case the customer is always informed of the decision).	**4.13.1 General** The following procedure provides for the control of any nonconforming SciConnect Inc. product or subcontracted items incorporated into SciConnect products.
4.13.2 Review and Disposition of Nonconforming Product As with other paragraphs, procedures are required to define "the responsibility for review and authority for the disposition of nonconforming product." This would involve, among other things, the following activities. • Description of the nature of nonconformity		**4.13.2 Review and Disposition of Nonconforming Product** Receiving inspection is responsible for identifying any nonconformities found during receiving inspection. Operators, in-process assemblers, machinists, and final inspectors are responsible for identifying all other nonconformities.

ISO 9001 or ISO 9002 Requirements	ABC Dry Cleaning	SciConnect, Inc.
and nature of repair is recorded. • Repair that does not conform to predetermined specified requirements must be reported for customer concessions. • Repaired and/or reworked product is reinspected.		All nonconformities are entered on the nonconformity form. The above-mentioned individuals have the authority to review and dispose of the nonconformance. Reworked items that require inspection shall be reinspected.
4.14 Corrective and Preventive Action	**4.14 Corrective and Preventive Action**	**4.14 Corrective and Preventive Action** The following procedure addresses corrective and preventive action. Prior to investigating a corrective or preventive action, the individual or team responsible for the analysis shall, whenever possible and with the support of data, estimate and record the cost and benefit associated with the action. If the benefits are deemed to outweigh the implementation cost, appropriate actions as described in 4.14.2 and 4.14.3 are implemented.
4.14.2 Corrective Action The procedure shall include • Effective handling of customer complaints • Investigation of the cause of nonconformity and recording of results of investigation	**4.14.2 Corrective Action** All customer complaints are handled by the owner or the assistant manager. Complaints are entered by the owner in the Customer Complaints Logbook and are reviewed and evaluated (as to the type of com-	**4.14.2 Corrective Action** Corrective actions can originate from a variety of internal and external sources, such as customer complaints (often resulting from an incorrect application), suppliers, internal quality audits, and employee sugges-

ISO 9001 or ISO 9002 Requirements	ABC Dry Cleaning	SciConnect, Inc.
• Determination of the corrective action needed to eliminate the cause of nonconformity • Assurance that corrective action is effective	plaint and whether or not it is a recurring complaint) once a month with the staff during regular end-of-the-month meeting. All employees are encouraged to submit suggestions. Suggestions are evaluated by the staff and the best potential candidate is tested. If the corrective action proves to be effective, it is implemented as a new procedure by the staff.	tions. Customer complaints resulting from the misapplication of a product are treated as corrective action. Once approved for investigation, a corrective action is investigated until the root cause is found and eliminated. All employees have been trained in problem-solving techniques and are encouraged to use these skills to eliminate the cause of nonconformity. Solution(s) to corrective actions are implemented and tested for effectiveness by the internal quality audit team. Records of all activities relating to the corrective action process are maintained in a file and are periodically reviewed by management.
4.14.3 Preventive Action The supplier must • Detect, analyze, and eliminate potential causes of nonconformities. • Initiate preventive action. • Ensure that relevant information on action taken is submitted for management review.	**4.14.3 Preventive Action** Process improvements and preventive action suggestions are achieved on a continuous basis through daily interactions with management and the staff.	**4.14.3 Preventive Action** The same principles outlined in 4.14.2 apply to the preventive action process. Corrective and preventive action requiring process changes is submitted to the responsible manager for proper documentation update.

ISO 9001 or ISO 9002 Requirements	ABC Dry Cleaning	SciConnect, Inc.
4.15 Handling, Storage, Packaging, Preservation, and Delivery The intent of these paragraphs is to ensure that the product is handled, packaged, and preserved in such a way as to prevent damage or deterioration. In addition, the standard requires that the supplier assesses, at appropriate intervals, the condition of product in storage for possible deterioration. Similar requirements cover packaging and delivery.	**4.15 Handling, Storage, Packaging, Preservation, and Delivery** **4.15.1 General** The following is ABC Dry Cleaning procedure. **4.15.2 Handling** All clothes are handled in such a way as to prevent damage. Expensive garments are handled with extra care. **4.15.3 Storage** Incoming product is stored in the storage cabinet. Since these products require no special handling and are not subject to deterioration, the condition of product in stock need not be assessed. **4.15.4 Packaging** ABC Dry Cleaning does not package clothes. Clothes are hung on hangers and individually wrapped in plastic bags.	**4.15 Handling, Storage, Packaging, Preservation, and Delivery** **4.15.1 General** The following procedures are written to address handling, storage, packaging, preservation, and delivery. **4.15.2 Handling** With the exception of columns, none of SciConnect Inc's products require special handling. Columns are handled with extra care and require no special training. **4.15.3 Storage** All receiving materials and finished goods are stored in a climate-controlled environment and require no special storage requirements. Receiving materials cannot be stored or stocked until they have been released by receiving inspection. Goods are stored on a first-in-first-out basis. All products are inventoried long before any physical deterioration is possible. **4.15.4 Packaging** Special customer packaging or routing instructions are written on the work order and entered in the computer. All oth-

ISO 9001 or ISO 9002 Requirements	ABC Dry Cleaning	SciConnect, Inc.
		er product is packaged in regular cardboard with either foam protection or Styrofoam shells. All necessary delivery instructions and marking are included on labels.
	4.15.5 Preservation	**4.15.5 Preservation**
	Preservation from dust is ensured by wrapping each garment in a plastic bag. No other form of preservation is required.	Preservation is not a particular problem for plastic components. All components are packaged in plastic bags to prevent dust.
	4.15.6 Delivery	**4.15.6 Delivery**
	Clothes coming from other stores are picked up by the delivery truck from the respective store.	All packages are delivered by a national (ISO 9002–certified) courier service or the customer's preferred courier.
	Clothes submitted by the customer are picked up by the customer or a representative.	
4.16 Control of Quality Records	**4.16 Control of Quality Records**	**4.16 Control of Quality Records**
Quality records, including subcontractor's records, must be maintained to demonstrate conformance to specified requirements and the effective operation of the quality system. These records must be stored in such a way as to prevent damage or deterioration and must be retained for a period of	ABC Dry Cleaning does not subcontract its work. Quality records consist of receipts on which the number of items received and special instructions are recorded, purchase orders for chemicals and other so-called receiving materials, customer complaints logged in a notebook, and results of internal	All records relating to this quality assurance system (supplier evaluation, inspection records, internal audit records, contract reviews, engineering reviews, etc.), are stored in the appropriate department. Records are maintained on-site for six months after which time they are archived on-site and re-

ISO 9001 or ISO 9002 Requirements	ABC Dry Cleaning	SciConnect, Inc.
time to be determined by the supplier.	quality audits conducted twice a year. All records are collected, filled, and stored by the owner for a period of one year after which time they are archived for a period of seven years solely for tax purposes.	tained for legal purposes for a period of seven years.
4.17 Internal Quality Audits Formal and documented audits of the quality system must be conducted at prescribed intervals by personnel independent of the activity being audited. Corrective actions must be addressed by the appropriate management. Follow-up activities are required to verify effectiveness of implementation.	**4.17 Internal Quality Audits** The effectiveness and suitability of the quality assurance system described in this document is monitored on a daily basis via constant inputs and interaction with the staff. Besides these daily interactions, the system is formally audited twice a year (May and October) by the owner. Records of the audits, corrective actions, and follow-up are maintained by the owner (see also 4.13 and 4.14).	**4.17 Internal Quality Audits** Internal quality audits for half of the quality system are conducted every six months. The selection the ISO 9001 paragraph that is audited is left to the discretion of the audit team, which consists of two SciConnect Inc. employees (six employees have been trained as internal auditors.) The results of internal audits are recorded using the internal audit form. A copy of the result is sent to the appropriate manager. Should corrective action(s) be required, a mutually agreed upon date will be negotiated by both parties. It is suggested that corrective actions must be resolved within 30 working days from the date of issue. Follow-up audits will verify the effectiveness of the corrective actions.

ISO 9001 or ISO 9002 Requirements	ABC Dry Cleaning	SciConnect, Inc.
		All audit reports are reviewed by the president of SciConnect Inc.
4.18 Training	**4.18 Training**	**4.18 Training**
The training needs of persons performing activities affecting quality shall be identified. Education, experience, or training are recognized by the standard. Records of training must be maintained.	All operations performed at ABC Dry Cleaning require little training. If a person does not have the experience to perform a specific task, the owner or an employee with experience will explain the process and monitor the trainee until that person is deemed properly trained. A record of the training process is maintained in the employee's file.	All employees receive a minimum of two days of on-the-job awareness training. During that period, employees are exposed to the activities of inspection, purchasing, sales, and assembly and testing. Professional training is also encouraged and financed by SciConnect Inc. Records of all training activities are available from the human resources department.
4.19 Servicing	**4.19 Servicing**	**4.19 Servicing**
If servicing (that is, product maintenance) is required, procedures must define specific servicing requirements.	ABC Dry Cleaning does not service its product. Hence this paragraph is not applicable.	SciConnect Inc. does not service its product, however it does provide its customers with technical advice, a form of servicing.
4.20 Statistical Techniques	**4.20 Statistical Techniques**	**4.20 Statistical Techniques**
The supplier must identify the need for statistical techniques and must establish procedures to implement and control the application of the identified statistical techniques.	After conducting a study of the potential benefits of applying statistical techniques to the various processes, ABC Dry Cleaning has come to the conclusion that such techniques would serve little purpose and will not help improve process capability.	

ISO 9001 or ISO 9002 Requirements	ABC Dry Cleaning	SciConnect, Inc.
		4.20.1 Identification of need The need for statistical techniques has been identified in tubing where an automated statistical process control (SPC) system has been implemented to verify process capability. **4.20.2 Procedures** The SPC procedures, including sampling frequency, are programmed in the statistical software package managed by the trained engineer in charge of the equipment.

Conclusions

Before concluding, I would like to share this story about ABC Dry Cleaning. Approximately two months after I had first drafted this chapter, my wife sent one of her favorite jackets to be dry cleaned (a stain had appeared on the right pocket). When she collected the jacket, she was horrified to find that the jacket had shrunk considerably and was not wearable. Fortunately for the owner, the jacket was not particularly expensive. When she asked the owner what had happened, he confessed that when he tried to remove the stain a halo developed around it and he had no choice but to wash the jacket and hope for the best! Naturally, the jacket shrank. The owner paid the cost of the jacket by offering "free" dry cleaning.

Had ABC Dry Cleaning been ISO 9002 registered, the problem would probably still have occurred; however, one would hope that it would be documented in a corrective action report. Was the wrong stain remover used? Was the person properly trained to use the stain remover? Was too much solvent used? How many similar problems occurred in the past? Is it more likely to occur with a particular type of fabric? Is it more likely to occur with a particular solvent? I doubt that these questions were asked, and it is likely that a few more jackets will shrink in the future. Still, if the risk of jackets shrinking is very low, that is, occurs very rarely, maybe implementing a corrective action is not necessary. Of course, the occurrence rate of a problem is not really an appropriate measure; cost per occurrence would more adequately assess the magnitude of the problem.

These case studies have helped us review the requirements of the ISO 9001 and ISO 9002 standards. I hope the sample text will assist you when you adapt your company's quality assurance system to the ISO 9000 series of standards. Having reviewed how requirements to the ISO 9001 standard can be addressed, we must now turn our attention to issues relating to the quality assurance system in general.

4   The ISO 9001 Standard as an Adaptable Quality Assurance System

The purpose of this chapter is to offer some suggestions on how to implement a quality assurance system that will both satisfy the standards and be easy to maintain—important criteria often overlooked by those newly introduced to ISO 9000.

A Typical Quality Assurance System

Figure 4.1 summarizes some of the basic activities found in most organizations, large or small. Naturally, not all activities would be found in all businesses. For example, since installation and servicing is often not performed by the manufacturer or assembler of a product but is often subcontracted to a third party, I have included the activity in parentheses. Similarly, not every organization has a laboratory to conduct tests or analyses. Paragraphs 4.1, Management Responsibility, 4.5, Document and Data Control, and 4.17, Internal Quality Audits, have been included outside the boundary to suggest that these paragraphs encompass the whole quality assurance system and therefore everything, including documents, that is contained within the box.

The numbers found in each box (4.3, 4.6, 4.9, and so on) represent the ISO 9001 paragraph number(s) likely to be associated with each activity. Some of the boxes are joined by bidirectional arrows to indicate possible interaction between departments. For example, marketing and/or sales employees, which are likely to be responsible for the implementation of paragraph 4.3, often interact with engineers to determine whether or not specific customer requirements can be achieved. Engineers, in turn, should interact with the manufacturing engineering department or process engineering department to further verify if certain requirements are achievable. You will notice that I did not say that engineering will or must interact with the process engineer or manufacturing engineer. I merely wrote that engineering *should* interact. Indeed, the ISO 9001 standard (and ISO 9002 or ISO 9003), does not specify which departments should interact with each other in order to satisfy customer requirements. Subparagraph 4.3.2c simply states that orders shall be reviewed to ensure that "the supplier has the capability to meet the contract or accepted order requirements." In addition, the supplier should ensure that

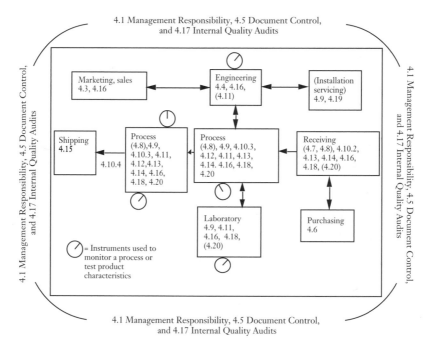

Figure 4.1. Correlation between ISO 9001 paragraphs and typical activities.

4.1	Management responsibility	4.7	Control of customer-supplied product
4.1.1	Quality policy		
4.1.2	Organization	4.8	Product identification and traceability
4.1.2.1	Responsibility and authority		
		4.9	Process control
4.1.2.2	Resources	4.10	Inspection and testing
4.1.2.3	Management representative	4.10.1	General
		4.10.2	Receiving inspection and testing
4.1.3	Management review		
4.2	Quality system	4.10.3	In-process inspection and testing
4.2.1	General		
4.2.2	Quality-system procedures	4.10.4	Final inspection and testing
4.2.3	Quality planning		
4.3	Contract review	4.10.5	Inspection and test records
4.3.1	General	4.11	Control of inspection, measuring, and test equipment
4.3.2	Review		
4.3.3	Amendment to a contract		
4.3.4	Records	4.11.1	General
4.4	Design control	4.11.2	Control procedure
4.4.1	General	4.12	Inspection and test status
4.4.2	Design and development planning	4.13	Control of nonconforming product
4.4.3	Organizational and technical interfaces	4.13.1	General
		4.13.2	Review and disposition of nonconforming product
4.4.4	Design input		
4.4.5	Design output	4.14	Corrective and preventive action
4.4.6	Design review		
4.4.7	Design verification	4.14.1	General
4.4.8	Design validation	4.14.2	Corrective action
4.4.9	Design changes	4.14.3	Preventive action
4.5	Document and data control	4.15	Handling, storage, packaging, reservation and delivery
4.5.1	General		
4.5.2	Document and data approval and issue	4.15.1	General
		4.15.2	Handling
4.5.3	Document and data changes	4.15.3	Storage
		4.15.4	Packaging
4.6	Purchasing	4.15.5	Preservation
4.6.1	General	4.15.6	Delivery
4.6.2	Evaluation of subcontractors	4.16	Control of quality records
		4.17	Internal quality audits
4.6.3	Purchasing data	4.18	Training
4.6.4	Verification of purchased product	4.19	Servicing
		4.20	Statistical techniques
4.6.4.1	Supplier verification at subcontractor's premise	4.20.1	Identification of need
		4.20.2	Procedures
4.6.4.2	Customer verification of subcontracted product		

Figure 4.1. *(continued)*

amendments to a contract are "correctly transferred to the functions concerned" (4.3.3). How you satisfy this requirement is up to you and will depend on the nature of the contract. For example, if a customer orders a standard product from a catalog, engineering will not need to intervene. If, however, a customer wishes to have a standard item customized to suit a unique need, then it is likely that engineering will be asked to review and comment on the proposed customizing to determine whether or not the order can be satisfactorily completed.

When Is a Requirement Not Required?

Some paragraphs, such as 4.7, Control of Customer-Supplied Product, 4.8, Product Identification and Traceability, 4.11, Control of Inspection, Measuring, and Test Equipment, and 4.20, Statistical Techniques, have been included in parentheses simply because the activity may not be performed or may be optional. For many companies, customers do not provide product(s) to be incorporated into the final product. For example, a company might manufacture a microchip to be incorporated onto a computer board manufactured by a supplier who inserts the board into a computer and sells it to a customer. A truck manufacturer might have to install tires provided by a customer. In such cases, customer-supplied products must be verified much as any other incoming raw material or subcomponent (see 4.7). Therefore, the requirements stated in paragraph 4.7 do not need to be addressed. I do, however, recommend that you briefly explain why in your quality manual. (See case studies found in chapter 3 for some examples.) If a customer provides you with fixtures, molds, or equipment to manufacture the product, then the paragraph cannot be ignored.

Traceability and Identification (4.8) is one of the few "where appropriate" paragraphs left within the standard. Since the requirement for traceability and product identification depends on the product (regulated or nonregulated) and customer requirements, companies have a broad range of options regarding the implementation of this paragraph (see examples provided in chapter 3).

Paragraph 4.11, Control of Inspection, Measuring, and Test Equipment, is not an optional paragraph, but its application depends greatly on the extent of measurements and testing being conducted. The significance of paragraph 4.11 to ABC Dry Cleaner and SciConnect Inc. will obviously be very different. I have included the paragraph in parentheses within the engineering function because engineering may (should) be involved in determining the type of measurement accuracy required for key parameters (this is specifically required by paragraph 4.11.2a). For example, engineering will often identify within a drawing certain parameters as key or crucial characteristics (paragraph 4.9d refers to these key parameters). Often, these parameters have tight tolerances (the two events of criticality and tight tolerance are not necessarily correlated). Given this scenario, how does one ensure that the equipment selected to monitor the tolerance in question has the required precision? Specifically, if a key characteristic is supposed to be machined and therefore measured to within $\frac{1}{1000}$ of an inch, how does one know that the instrument used (micrometer or caliper) is sufficiently precise to measure to within $\frac{1}{1000}$ of an inch? In fact, certain guidelines would recommend that the instrument be 10 times more precise than the specified tolerance (that is, accurate to within $\frac{1}{10,000}$ of an inch). Such requirements for gauge or equipment capability are routinely required of suppliers to the automotive industry. If the equipment is new and properly maintained and operated, one could rely on the certificate provided by the equipment manufacturer. If these conditions do not apply, the only way to ascertain the instrument's precision is to conduct a costly repeatability and reproducibility study for each instrument (known as gauge R&R studies). Luckily, software is available to conduct such studies.

Paragraph 4.20, Statistical Techniques, is listed in parentheses within some of the boxes because one does not need to conduct statistical studies for all processes. The laboratory could use various techniques such as SPC to monitor the precision of its instruments. Receiving inspection could rely on acceptance sampling techniques to monitor suppliers, and a host of techniques could be used throughout the various processes to monitor certain process parameters. One must realize that the (statistical) monitoring of some parameters may not be practical, efficient, or feasible in all cases. If, for example, a company produces four or five multimillion dollar products a year, the use of statistical techniques would be impossible to apply effectively even if so-called short-run techniques are used. In other cases, especially where the customer does require that the use of statistical techniques be demonstrated or where the process technology is already well-established and proven or in instances where the processes are rather simple and straightforward, the use of statistical techniques would be of dubious value. Paragraph 4.20 of the standard does not specifically state that the supplier must be able to demonstrate that the processes are statistically capable, however the requirement for "establishing, controlling and verifying process capability and product characteristics" does come very close to suggesting that techniques such as SPC or similar techniques be used (the ISO 9004 guidelines document does suggest the use of SPC and other techniques). Therefore, whenever possible, particularly if required by the customer, the use of statistical techniques should be identified in order to assess whether or not processes are (statistically) capable.

Interrelationship Between Paragraphs

An occasional mistake made by some ISO 9000 novices is to assume that each paragraph is independent of the other. Nothing could be further from the truth. There is a lot of interconnection between paragraphs, as Figure 4.2 illustrates.

Starting with subparagraph 4.9d, let us explain some of the actual or potential or implied connections between paragraphs. Subparagraph 4.9d states that the supplier needs to consider the "monitoring and control of suitable process parameters and product characteristics." What does that mean?

Figure 4.3 is a schematic representation of a generic process referred to as process A. The process consists of many subprocesses and sub-subprocesses (see legend of figure). Each subprocess can be defined by a series of key process characteristics or parameters that are deemed important enough to require monitoring and ensure product quality as *expected or defined* by the customer (see paragraph 4.3, Contract Review). The legend within Figure 4.3 lists a few examples of key process parameters for the fictitious process 6a. Each industry has,

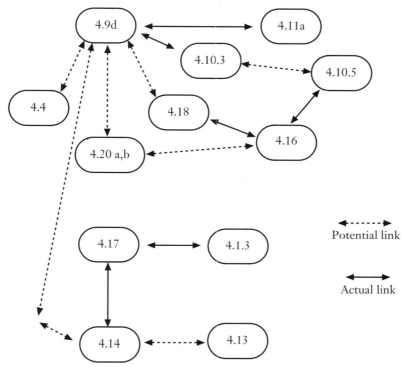

Figure 4.2. Interrelationship between some ISO 9001 paragraphs.

over the years, identified its own list of key process parameters that require careful monitoring.

Let us assume that you have defined a set of key parameters that are crucial to your processes (and thus worth monitoring) in order to ensure product quality as expected by your customers. Let us refer to these key characteristics as A, B, and C. How do you ensure that characteristics A, B, and C are controlled? Of course, there are several ways to ensure control. Within the manufacturing or assembly world, most organizations monitor and control their key characteristics by purchasing equipment or complex systems that measure the characteristics in question and ensure that their values do not deviate

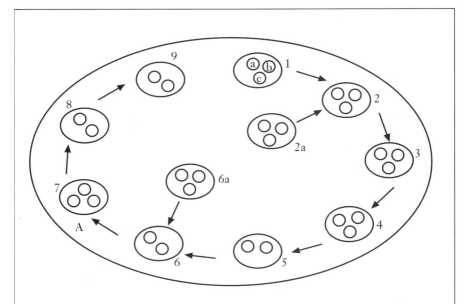

The above generic process, labeled A, could represent any process: building a truck, providing a service, or a variety of other processes. As with any process, process A consists of several sub-processes (1–9), each in turn consisting of anywhere between two to three sub-subprocesses (a–c). Each of these subprocesses may have some key characteristics or parameters that are defined either by engineering, manufacturing, marketing/sales, the customer, or a combination of all of the above.

 Subprocess 6a consists of three subprocesses. Each of these subprocesses may be defined by a few key (or important) characteristics. Examples of key characteristics found in the manufacturing/assembly world would include: temperature, pressure, torque, acidity (pH), current, voltage, inside or outside diameter length, weight, flow rate, conductivity, and hundreds of other measures.

Figure 4.3. A generic view of a process and key characteristics.

between certain predetermined ranges. If the characteristic in question (A, B, or C) deviates beyond a certain range, one can then adjust/control the characteristic by applying some corrective action (opening/closing a valve, increasing the temperature, adjusting the acidity, or a multitude of other adjustments). We have now established a link between paragraph 4.9c and 4.11.2a. Paragraph 4.11.2a states that

> The supplier shall: a) determine the measurements to be made and the accuracy required, and select the appropriate inspection, measuring, and test equipment that is capable of the necessary accuracy and precision.

In other words, once you have determined that certain product characteristics are worth monitoring, which usually, *but not always*, means measuring, then you must ensure that the instrument performing the measurement is accurate and precise enough to measure variation which might eventually affect product quality.

The other links (implied or direct) are easier to explain. Paragraph 4.10.3, In-Process Inspection and Testing, is a logical extension of 4.9d. In-process inspection or testing requires in turn that quality records be kept, hence the connection with paragraph 4.10.5, Inspection and Test Records and 4.16, Control of Quality Records. Paragraphs 4.4, Design Control and 4.20, Statistical Techniques, are logical extensions, however, they are not necessarily linked to 4.9d or the other subparagraphs of 4.9. Yet, it is typical for engineering or for manufacturing engineering and design engineering to define the key characteristics and their maximum or safe operational ranges; thus the connection between 4.4 and 4.9d. It is not unusual for process engineers or quality engineers to monitor key process parameters or characteristics by using various statistical techniques to determine whether or not the parameter or characteristic in question is in statistical control. Whenever these techniques are used, the individual in charge of applying and maintaining the appropriate statistical technique(s) will require adequate education and/or training (hence the link with paragraphs 4.20.2 and 4.18. Finally, any statistical recording or collection of data relating to the monitoring of key process parameters will likely be subject to the requirements of paragraph 4.16,

Control of Quality Records, and paragraph 4.5, Document and Data Control. See if you can explain why the remaining paragraphs of Figure 4.2 are connected.

Controlling the Quality Manual

The structure of the sample quality manuals found in chapter 3 duplicates the structure of the ISO 9001 standard. Naturally, you do not have to follow this approach. You could, for example, provide the reader with a concordance matrix. But I highly recommend following the standard because it is easier to audit, and most auditors will appreciate the format.

Technically speaking, the examples in chapter 3 do not yet constitute a proper quality manual. This could easily be achieved by adopting the following three steps.

1. Include a cover page and decide how you will control revisions. There is no need to come up with elaborate revision numbers. I have seen too many manuals with complicated revisions and control schemes requiring up to 15 signatures per approval. Such methods are not appropriate for small businesses and are not required by the ISO 9000 standards. I strongly suggest that you make use of the many tools already available in software. All word processors will allow you to create various style sheets in which you can include textual information, dates, and even hour of day. Do not complicate your life; use a simple template sheet. The sample shown would be adequate.

| Quality Manual for ABC Dry Cleaning | Issued: February 13, 1995 |
| | Previous issue: Feb. 21, 1993 |

2. As an optional requirement, you might want to insert a one-page description of your company (type of business, years in business, and so on.) Some companies even insert a high-level flow diagram describing their major processes. This information is not really required by any of the ISO 9000 series of standards, but is helpful to your customers and third-party auditors.

3. Decide how the manual will be controlled and by whom. This is an important step. You have a couple of options; you could do either

of the following:

a. Have the president/owner of the company approve the whole manual by signing the title page or an introductory statement. By signing the manual, the president approves the quality assurance system described in the quality manual. (Note: Signatures become irrelevant if the manual is to be maintained in a master computer file. In such cases, various systems of passwords or read/write protect options could be implemented to allow only approved personnel to modify the document[s].)

b. You could have each manager approve/sign the appropriate sections of the quality manual and the president of the company would then approve the whole manual. This approach is more tedious and a bit more difficult to control, but in small companies, the process should not be difficult to manage.

A sample page for ABC Dry Cleaning is reproduced in Figure 4.4. The whole manual would consist of an additional 15–20 pages approved by the owner or president.[1] I also recommend that you define, within the introduction of the manual, the type of products you manufacture, service, or assemble; their application(s); and/or your customer base. This is important because it allows you to identify the scope and nature of your business. The following paragraph is an example.

> **Introduction**
> XYZ Inc. stores and distributes ammonia, treated ammonium nitrate, and urea ammonium nitrate. These products are sold to local farmers or co-ops for farming and agricultural applications.

The introduction does not have to be more than a few sentences long. The example identifies the main function of the plant ("stores and distributes"), the type of products, and the community of customers. One could also list the applications for the product(s)—for example, water treatment, refrigeration, purification, heat treatment, and so on.

Quality Manual for ABC Dry Cleaning	Issued: February 13, 1995
	Previous issue: Feb. 21, 1993

4.1 Management Responsibility
4.1.1 Quality Policy

The owner and staff of ABC Dry Cleaning are committed to maintaining customer satisfaction. This is achieved by ensuring that all items brought to our store for dry cleaning are processed as per customer requirements and are handled with the greatest of care throughout all of our processes.

Our customer satisfaction is monitored on an ongoing basis by routinely asking all of our customers whether their previous order was handled and processed to their satisfaction.

Should items be damaged within our facilities, ABC Dry Cleaning will perform all necessary repairs before delivery and at no charge to the customer.

4.1.2 Organization
4.1.2.1 Responsibility and Authority

All employees of ABC Dry Cleaning have the authority to initiate corrective and preventive actions relating to product or process nonconformities.

Recommendations or suggestions can be submitted to management for approval by all employees.

A review of records relating to product nonconformities is conducted bimonthly (or more frequently if need be) by the whole staff to determine whether or not changes to the quality system should be implemented (see 4.14).

The effectiveness of suggested solutions is monitored during our quarterly internal assessment process (see 4.17), until cause(s) for nonconformities is/are properly identified.

Figure 4.4. A sample page of the ABC Dry Cleaning quality manual.

Conclusions

As with any system, a quality assurance system consists of interrelated parts or subcomponents that function as a whole. Changes in one subcomponent (a procedure, a method, or a department) may impact another component. One of the challenges of implementing an ISO 9000 quality assurance system is to try to develop a system that will maintain flexibility and minimize the potential impact of changes on other components. This can be achieved, in part, by designing simple forms and procedures. Since you will have to write procedures and use forms to record results, the next chapter explores how you can address these issues.

Note

1. A software package (ISOFT) designed to help you write a quality manual is available from the author at phone number 206-644-9504, fax number 206-644-9524.

5   Designing Forms and Writing Procedures

In my capacity as an ISO 9000 lead assessor over the past six years, I have seen hundreds of forms: complicated forms, long forms, small forms, simple forms, controlled forms, uncontrolled forms, red forms, green forms, pink forms, brown forms, and just about every other color. Reviewing them all, I have often noticed that spaces or blocks within a form are rarely or never filled in. Forms requiring four signatures only have one or none. When I ask people why the information required by the form is not collected, I am told that the information is either no longer required or only required in special/ rare cases, or the person simply does not know why the information is requested or what is the nature of the information.

This chapter provides more detailed examples on how procedures can be written to satisfy specific ISO 9001 or ISO 9002 requirements while at the same time meet specific business needs. Examples are not provided for every one of the ISO 9001 paragraphs, but you should be able to develop other procedures using the examples found in this chapter.

On Forms

Since forms are usually used to record verbal and/or numerical information (data), they are an integral part of the quality assurance system and are required to satisfy the many references to quality records found within the ISO 9000 series of standards (see, for example, paragraph 4.16). Arguments vary as to whether or not forms should be under document control. I know some auditors who would get particularly upset if they were to find uncontrolled forms during an audit. In my opinion, a form is not necessarily a document, yet some dictionaries define a form as a type of document. So the question remains, if forms are considered to be documents, should they necessarily be controlled as specified by paragraph 4.5, Document and Data Control, of ISO 9001, ISO 9002, or ISO 9003? I believe the answer is no, because forms are not likely to affect the quality of a product. A form is a piece of paper used to record information that may or may not be part of the quality assurance system. Thus, a filled-out form is a record and records do not have to be controlled, at least not in the sense of paragraph 4.5. Nevertheless, forms may exist that may have to be controlled. If, for example, a form includes equations, formulas, or other instructions necessary to perform a test, then the form could be conceived to be a document that should be under document control.

I present yet another argument to demonstrate that forms are not necessarily documents subject to the requirements of document control. Read paragraphs 4.5.2 and 4.5.3 and replace the word *documents* with the word *forms*. Do the paragraphs make sense, and, more importantly, would such action add value to your organization? After rereading the paragraphs, your conclusion may well be that forms are not to be viewed as documents. But, if you disagree, you must then make sure that

- Forms are reviewed and approved for adequacy by authorized personnel.
- Appropriate forms are available at all locations.
- Invalid and obsolete forms are promptly removed from all points of issue.

- Obsolete forms retained for legal and/or knowledge-preservation purposes are suitably identified.

If you do not currently have forms (which is unlikely), or if you need to upgrade your forms, I offer some suggestions. To begin, avoid copying someone else's form. A form and the information collected on it are specific to a company and the type of product(s) it manufactures or services it provides. Forms designed for a specific application or specific industry are not necessarily suited for all other industries.

When you design a form, design it in such a way to collect only the information that is required (or is required to be collected by your customers or regulatory agencies). The information that you collect should be of value to you. The best way to design a form is to first design a simple format, collect only what is absolutely necessary, and then test the form's effectiveness by trying it for a few weeks. You may find out that you need to collect more information, or you may want to delete information that you thought was essential but turns out to be of little value. If, after a trial of a few weeks, you find out that certain sections of the forms are left blank or are rarely used, it is likely that the information is not necessary. Perhaps the information could be captured in a comment section. Once the form is tested and approved, print as many as you need. (Unfortunately the reverse process tends to occur: the form is designed, thousands of copies are printed, and thousands of corrections or misapplications soon follow.) You may also have to train people on how to use the form correctly. This is rarely, if ever, done. In many cases there is a good reason why a particular item is included in a form and only the person who designed the form knows why. Once that person is gone, no one seems to remember why the item was included.

Suppose your company does not currently have a form that will allow you to control nonconforming products, as required by paragraph 4.13 of ISO 9001 or ISO 9002. Let us review what would be needed. The paragraph (4.13.1) specifies that we should be able to identify, document, evaluate, segregate (when practical), disposit the nonconforming product, and notify concerned parties. In addition, paragraph 4.13.2 states that

- The person who has the responsibility for reviewing the nonconformance should be identified.

- The nonconformance review should follow a procedure.

- If the supplier is required to obtain a concession from the customer, the description of the nonconformity that has been accepted and (necessary) repairs shall be recorded to denote the actual condition (of the product).

- Finally, repaired and/or reworked product shall be reinspected in accordance with the quality plan or documented procedures.

Figure 5.1 is an example of a blank form to control nonconforming products.

Paragraph 4.13.2 would require the following minimum information.

1. Product identification.

2. Description of the nonconformance.

3. Identification of the internal department or external function (for example, supplier or subcontractor) responsible for the nonconformance.

4. Determination of who will review the nonconformance for appropriate disposition, as well as determination whether or not customer concessions are required. (Note: Customer concessions are not required for all nonconformities. Indeed, customers usually do not want to be informed about nonconformities found during receiving inspection or in-process assemblies. These nonconformities are resolved by the supplier or subcontractor without having to inform the customer. Customers, however, may want to know about nonconformities discovered prior to shipping the product.)

5. Reinspection requirements for repaired or reworked product.

Figure 5.2 shows a completed form that is simple but identifies all that is required by paragraph 4.13. Naturally, the amount of space

---

Nonconforming Form

Work station:_____   Date:_____

Product identification: _____
Supplier (internal or external): _____
Description of nonconformance:

_____

_____

Disposition:

_____

_____

Reinspection: Required:_____   Not required: _____

Comments:

_____

_____

Reviewed and approved by: _____ Date: _____

Figure 5.1. Sample form for controlling nonconforming products.

allocated can be adjusted to suit the need of each company. Additional information can be added, but only if absolutely necessary.

On Procedures

Procedures are important; however, they will never prevent mishaps or strange scenarios, as the following examples illustrate. A friend of mine who suffers from a bad case of arthritis in his right knee decided

---

Nonconforming Form

Work station: AS-10   Date: Dec. 08, 1994

Product identification: Subassembly OP-132

Supplier (internal or external): (Internal) Work station AS-09

Description of nonconformance:

Subassembly OP-132 failed functional test ENG-12. (Note: Specific details of the failure could be included.)

Disposition:

Unit was reviewed by test engineering, and it was determined that the wrong test procedure was applied. ENG-21 instead of ENG-12 should have been used. Error was due to a typographical error on work order. Subassembly passed test ENG-21.

Reinspection: Required:_____ Not required:___x___

Comments:

_____

_____

Reviewed and approved by: Jane Rich (QA manager)
Date: Dec. 9, 94

Figure 5.2. Completed form for controlling nonconforming products.

to have an operation. On the day of the operation, the anesthesiologist strolls in the operating room and says to my friend: "Good morning. I see that we are going to operate on your left knee."

"No," replied my friend, "it is the *right* knee."

"Are you sure? It says here on the chart, left knee."

"Of course I am sure! *It is my right knee!*"

Obviously, the form/record was wrong. Fortunately, the anesthesiologist decided to perform one final verification of the written record, just in case. Perhaps the procedure of verbally verifying with the patient (the customer) the nature of the operation was implemented after a few unfortunate errors were committed.[1]

In some cases the routine application of procedures can lead to ridiculous scenarios. I recently checked into a hotel where I was supposed to meet a friend who was also staying in the same hotel. As I began filling out the usual check-in form, I asked the attendant if there were any messages. "Yes," the woman replied, "a gentleman was just asking if you had checked in."

"That must have been Mr. Fitz," I replied.

"That is correct, sir."

"Could you tell me in what room Mr. Fitz is staying?"

"I am sorry, sir, it is against policy to give that information."

I find such replies rather amusing. The clerk had clearly established that Mr. Fitz knew me and was looking for me. Moreover, I had confirmed that I expected a message from Mr. Fitz, and yet, I had to first call the hotel's operator to be connected with Mr. Fitz. I suppose security procedures are security procedures, irrespective of the situation (that is the problem with some procedures; they on occasion replace common sense).

This last example is a clear case of the failure of procedures. Some friends had ordered two items: a leather sofa with back support and a piece of oak furniture. Some 30 days later, the items were finally delivered: the furniture was made of white wood (not oak), and the sofa had no special back support. When my friends complained, the deliveryman assured them that there was no problem returning the furniture. "But there is a problem," my friend tried to explain. "We have had to wait 30 days for a wrong delivery. Besides, it says right here on the purchase order: oak and special back support." The deliveryman agreed that someone had made a mistake. It would appear that someone had not read the special instructions and/or chose to ignore them—hoping that the customer, having already waited 30 days for the delivery, would accept what was delivered rather than what was ordered.

Perhaps the best way to illustrate how not to write a procedure is with the following example.

Example of a Bad Engineering Procedure. The following example is intended to be an amusing and fictitious engineering procedure written by an unknown, but astute, source.

Engineering desk procedure 105-705-1022/02-1995
for the calculation of 1 + 1

Every new engineer must learn early that it is never good taste to designate the sum of two quantities in the form

$$1 + 1 = 2 \tag{1}$$

Anyone who has made a study of advanced mathematics is aware that

$$1 = \ln e$$

$$1 = \sin^2 x + \cos^2 x$$

Furthermore

$$2 = \sum_{n=0}^{\infty} \left(\frac{1}{2}\right)^n$$

Therefore, equation (1) can be expressed more scientifically as

$$\ln e + (\sin^2 x + \cos^2 x) = \sum_{n=0}^{\infty} \left(\frac{1}{2}\right)^n \tag{2}$$

This may be further simplified by use of the following relations

$$1 = \cosh y \sqrt{1 - \tanh^2 y} \quad \text{and} \quad e = \lim_{z \to \infty} \left(1 + \frac{1}{z}\right)^z$$

Equation (2) may, therefore, be rewritten as

$$\ln\left[\lim_{z \to \infty}\left(1 + \frac{1}{z}\right)^z\right] + (\sin^2 x + \cos^2 x) = \sum_{n=0}^{\infty} \frac{\cosh y\sqrt{1 - \tanh^2 y}}{2^n} \qquad (3)$$

At this point, it should be obvious that equation (3) is much clearer and more easily understood than equation (1). Other methods of a similar nature could be used to clarify equation (1) but these are easily discovered once the reader grasps the underlying principles.

I do not know if this example has amused or frustrated you, but I can assure you that I have seen many procedures that are so complex and include so many steps (as many as 50 sometimes) that they make the facetious engineering procedure look simple by comparison. Individuals who waste their time writing procedures, reminiscent of the earlier mathematical tour de force, fail to consider that most individuals possess a certain level of education or knowledge, which, if inadequate to perform a specific task or job, can always be complemented with some additional training, which is precisely the intent of paragraph 4.18, Training.

In all of the examples, whether or not a procedure existed, the customer is still left either angry (wrong knee), dissatisfied (hotel), or very frustrated (furniture). Therefore, in order to be effective, procedures must be carefully written, wisely applied, and revised, and may not even be required if the individual has appropriate training. Or once written, procedures may require special training to ensure that they are followed properly.

Procedures tend to fall in one of two categories: they can either be detailed and allow for no deviation or flexibility, or allow for the user to use his or her own judgment. Some processes may require very detailed procedures that follow a well-defined sequence of events. These processes may require little training or may demand special technical skills (laboratory technician, for example). Other processes may only define a beginning and an end with no specified sequences in between. These processes may be performed by individuals with special education, skills, and training (chemists, programmers, engineers, or technicians, for example). In such cases, the knowledge and/or skills acquired during the educational or training process may already include standardized procedures. Chemists, for example, are trained how to perform basic operations and conduct experiments within a laboratory environment. One need not write a procedure for a chemist on how to run a titration or operate a pH meter. Trained machinists need not be told how to set up their lathes, numerically controlled lathes, or drills. Still, in many cases, operating procedures or work instructions need to be prepared in order for someone to perform a task or set of tasks.

Procedures: How to Write Them

With the exception of two paragraphs, 4.1, Management Responsibility, and 4.12, Inspection and Test Status, all other paragraphs of the ISO 9001–9003 standards begin with the following words: "The supplier shall establish and maintain documented procedures for . . ." Obviously, the need to develop procedures is difficult to avoid, but the standard does not specify how long or how detailed a procedure needs to be. Nor does it state that all procedures must be written. Indeed, several media and formats are available.

The traditional approach is to write procedures on paper. Since all procedures relating to the standards must be controlled (paragraph 4.5, Document and Data Control), people have found that as the number of procedures increases, the task of controlling these documents (ensuring that only the latest approved revision is available to all parties) becomes increasingly difficult. In an attempt to solve this problem, more and more companies have begun to rely on the use of computers and computer software databases to manage their documents and engineering drawings.

The advantage of using computers is that a master list of all documents with their revision status and location can easily be maintained in a computer database. Also, in small companies, revision control is easier to achieve simply because the responsibility to maintain the database can be assigned to one or two people. Computer files can be protected with a read-only status to prevent anyone other than approved individuals from writing onto the file and thus introducing unapproved modifications.

Companies wishing to utilize computers to store their procedures must also consider that unless they have enough personal computers networked together, the system will be of limited value. Certainly, if the only computers available are with managers and if no one else can access the information on the shop floor, then the system will be ineffective. Consequently, the use of computers to automate the documentation process assumes that enough computers will be available.

Procedures can also consist of diagrams, pictures, or videos. Flow diagrams are often used as a means to describe processes and interaction between processes (see Part II). The advantage of flow diagrams is that very little training is required to learn how to read them. Flow diagrams can also be used to train new employees or retrain employees about modified procedures. Finally, one of the advantages of using flowcharts to describe a process is that it allows individuals to review the process and suggest improvements. This opportunity to critically review and perhaps improve or reengineer, to use a trendy word of the early 1990s, a process (as it is being transferred onto a flow diagram) is often ignored.

Still, flowcharts should be used wisely and are not suitable for all applications. There are at least two problems with the use of flowcharts: (1) they tend to be overused, and (2) they usually provide the reader with a high-level (global) description. The application of flowcharts to describe every process referred to in the many paragraphs of the ISO 9000 models is sometimes encouraged by consultants. The result is a manual that consists of page after page of flowcharts that are of little value to anyone.

Another problem with flowcharts is that they can give the impression that a process is well thought-out when actually, upon closer inspection, they may represent nothing more than a schematic representation of a vague or ill-defined thought process. I once read a five-page flowchart describing design change control. One of the decision boxes listed on the third page had the following words: "Is general design review required?" As you read the flowchart, you still did not know who decided whether or not a design review process was required! What was needed was another subprocess (a lower-level flowchart) that would explain how this decision was achieved.

The process of documenting and flowcharting every activity is very expensive and of dubious value, since no one is likely to ever read the volumes of procedures that attempt to temporarily freeze the many operating systems. This attempt to document, in minute detail, every work instruction and/or process has been brought about by the comments of some ill-advised military auditors (and since repeated by some ISO 9000 auditors). These auditors love to ask the following question: "What will you do if Mr. Smith dies tomorrow?" The implication of this absurd remark is that one should have a documented system that would be so detailed as to include everything Mr. Smith ever knew about a particular job. What these auditors seem to forget is that it is impossible to document everything Mr. Smith ever knew about a process simply because, in most cases, that would lead to an incredibly long and complex set of procedures that no one could ever read. Moreover, if such procedures could ever be written and maintained, it would no doubt affect the cost of the final product.

Regardless of which media one uses to document a process, ensure that the procedure addresses the requirements listed within the standard. Let us examine the requirements for paragraph 4.13, for example. As you read paragraph 4.13, Control of Nonconforming Product, the first thing you notice is that the review for nonconforming products must be performed according to a documented procedure. It is not enough to have a form to record the information, you must also have a procedure that describes how nonconforming products are reviewed and how dispositions are achieved. The procedure need not be complicated; however, it should be written in such a way as to allow all types of nonconformances to be addressed. In fact, you may consider writing a brief generic procedure and design a form that will ensure that all the required steps are performed. As always, the standard is not specific and simply states that the documented procedure should "ensure that product that does not conform to specified requirements is prevented from unintended use or installation." You will recall that by product, the standard refers to intended product, the product that is either assembled or manufactured, or a service delivered by the company applying for ISO 9000 registration. Does this mean that product(s) incorporated within the intended product is/are not subject to nonconformity reviews? Of course not. Nonconformity reviews apply throughout the production processes, from product received during incoming inspection to in-process assemblies or manufacturing and final inspection and/or testing (if performed). Should nonconformity reviews cover administrative processes such as purchasing, marketing, or human resources? Not really; however, the practice of conducting nonconformity reviews for all processes could certainly benefit administrative processes.

Should all nonconformances be reviewed by the quality assurance department? Not necessarily. In writing a procedure, one must recognize that the responsibility and authority to review and resolve a nonconformance can be delegated and would depend on the type, frequency, and nature of the nonconformance. Many companies authorize their assemblers to record and resolve certain (so-called low level) nonconformances at the work station level. The quality manager (if such an individual exists) need not approve every action. The standard allows for flexibility and does not in any way suggest that all nonconformances must be reviewed by one individual or department.

Writing a Procedure to Address Specific Requirements

When writing a procedure, use common sense and don't promise what you can't deliver. Above all, describe what you are currently doing. If what you are currently doing does not make sense, then modify your procedure. Do not simply document a procedure that you know is inefficient or rarely followed. One of the advantages of implementing a quality assurance system that will comply with ISO 9001, ISO 9002, or ISO 9003 is that you have the opportunity to review and reassess the current efficiency and effectiveness of your processes and quality assurance system (assuming you have such a system). If you do not have a system in place, then the ISO 9000 series will provide you with the framework to develop one. Let us first review the intent and requirements of paragraph 4.13, Control of Nonconforming Product.

The standard intends that the company establish and maintain a documented procedure to ensure that any product that does not conform to specific requirements is prevented from unintended use or installation. Once a product has been identified as nonconforming, it must be identified (labeled or marked) and segregated, if possible. The nature of the nonconformity must also be evaluated and documented for eventual disposition (reworked, accepted as-is, regraded for other application, rejected, or scrapped). If needed, notification to the functions concerned must also be ensured. Finally, repaired and/or reworked product shall be reinspected.

The previous paragraph assumes that specific requirements have been written. But what requirements is the standard referring to? Customer requirements, requirements imposed on subcontractors or subsuppliers (your suppliers), internal requirements developed by the supplier to satisfy customer requirements, or everyone? And what about cases where the customer has only vague requirements, or no specific quantitative requirement? When trying to interpret the ISO 9000 standards, always remember that the standards' original intent (before they were to be applied to all industries including the service sector) applied to a product or products that was/were perceived to be either assembled, manufactured, or otherwise put together from other subassemblies, subcomponents, or services. Therefore, "specified requirements" originally meant any requirements relating to either customer requirements (if they existed), statutory requirements, or internal requirements developed with the intent to satisfy the customer's understanding of quality requirements no matter how vaguely defined these requirements might be. The term specification has now taken a new, expanded meaning and includes all sorts of specifications for tangible and nontangible products, such as consulting.

Consequently, you should carefully analyze what your current critical requirements are, define which ones are less critical or not critical at all, and develop a procedure that will cover all situations. In other words, before writing a procedure you must think about your current situation and the consequences of enforcing a particular procedure. If, as is the case for some processing industries, your processes can absorb a broad range of incoming raw materials or components without affecting the quality of the final product delivered to your customers, then you should write your procedure to reflect that fact.

For example, I once visited a chemical plant that produced fertilizer. After reviewing the specifications written for the incoming raw material (ammonium and natural gas), I learned that the specifications were really not all that important because the process could be adjusted (at some cost) to compensate for unacceptable variation in the specifications. As it turned out, the specifications were artificial. One manager pointed out that "with natural gas, we don't really know who the supplier is because, although Texaco provides us with the gas, it comes from many other sources and it would be impossible to trace the sources. Besides, if it has a bit too much sulphur [an important characteristic], we can't do anything about it, and it does not matter anyway because we have scrubbers to take care of that problem."[2] Obviously, in this situation the issue of nonconformity for raw material needs to be adapted to the needs of the industry.

Testing the Procedure

All too often, once a procedure is documented it is not rigorously implemented. This occurs because of a variety of reasons: a process has changed; the procedure is too complicated; a supplier quality program has improved, but the procedure was not adjusted to reflect the change; or a host of other reasons. To prevent this from occurring, periodically review your procedures to ensure they are relevant, suitable, and still effective.

Once a procedure has been written it must be validated by testing it for accuracy and suitability. One way to validate a procedure is to conduct internal audits of the quality assurance system. Too often, internal audits are used to merely find nonconformances and write nonconformance reports. Before long, the role and purpose of an audit(or) is perceived as an activity whose sole purpose is to ensure that procedures are meticulously followed. No wonder people do not like to be audited!

Internal audits, and I am referring to first-party audits (employees auditing their own company), should not be conducted solely to verify whether or not procedures are meticulously followed. They should be used as a means to test and verify the effectiveness of procedures. Internal audits are a great opportunity to improve procedures and/or processes. This does not mean that more procedures or longer procedures are better. Improvement may mean simplification. In cases where the employees have already received training, it might be better to write guidelines rather than procedures. Guidelines allow for flexibility and rely on the knowledge and expertise of the individual. Naturally, guidelines will not satisfy all situations. In some cases, detailed procedures, such as testing procedures, may well be required. Figures 5.3 through 5.7 show examples of procedures.

Control of Inspection, Measuring, and Test Equipment (4.11)

If you are calibrating your own instruments, consider what type of equipment and training is be required. In many cases, the calibration is rather simple and requires a simple zeroing of the instrument, but for more sophisticated instruments, such as a spectrometer, more skills are required.

There are several places to obtain standards to calibrate your instruments. Gauge blocks for micrometers and calipers are sold by a few companies. These blocks usually come with a certificate specifying the referenced national or international standard and the accuracy of the blocks and at what temperature range they are rated. (Note: For certain applications, the accuracy of the blocks may also have to be periodically verified.) Chemical standards may be purchased from national organizations or from certain industries that provide industry standards. In some cases, no standards (industry, national, or international) are available!

When calibrating an instrument, record the deviation (that is the actual reading). That information can be valuable months later. Do not simply say that the instrument was "okay." Recording the data will allow you to determine if you can open the calibration interval from one month to three months, for example. This ability to relax the calibration interval can save you money.

Whenever possible or desirable, calibrate your instrument at two extremes. For example, do not simply calibrate your pH meters at a

4.13   Control of Nonconforming Product at XYZ Inc.
4.13.1 General
Nonconforming product: A product is considered to be nonconforming if it does not satisfy any of the following conditions.

1. Violation of XYZ Inc. specifications listed, when required, on purchasing orders.

2. Data provided on the certificate of analysis does not agree with in-house analyses occasionally performed at random intervals.

3. Quantity ordered or time of delivery does not match contractual agreement.

The following procedure ensures that nonconforming product is removed from the process and reviewed by the appropriate party (defined below) for appropriate corrective action. The term *product* is meant to include not only all in-process units, but also most incoming products and subcontracted components that are assembled or otherwise incorporated within XYZ Inc. final products delivered to our customers. Exceptions to these conditions (especially with respect to incoming products) are noted on an as-required basis either on the purchasing order or the work order.

All nonconformities, irrespective of their origin, are documented on a nonconformity form (see sample). The nonconformity form defines the required steps.

4.13.2 Review and Disposition of Nonconforming Product
The responsibility and authority for the review of nonconforming product is assigned to two functions.

1. Incoming inspection, which notifies purchasing (see 4.6).

2. Operators who have received training to identify and/or recognize nonconformities during in-process or final inspection. Final decision regarding the approval of disposition will be rendered by the area supervisor (see operator training) or quality manager.

Nonconforming product can either be (a) repaired, (b) scrapped, or (c) accepted with or without concessions. Concessions can be submitted by the area supervisor or salesperson responsible for the order/product for final customer approval. Repaired units will be reinspected unless otherwise specified in the quality plan or contract. Records of reinspection are maintained by the area supervisor. A description of all nonconformities and dispositions are entered in the nonconformity database and are reviewed weekly during production meetings (see 4.14, Corrective and Preventive Action).

Cross-reference: Paragraph 4.6, Purchasing; 4.14, Corrective and Preventive Action; 4.16, Control of Quality Records; and 4.18, Training.

Figure 5.3. Sample procedure for nonconforming product (4.13).

4.14   Corrective and Preventive Action

4.14.1 General

The following procedure addresses requirements for corrective and preventive action resulting from customer complaints or any of the internal processes directly associated with the quality assurance system as defined in this quality manual. It is the responsibility of the appropriate manager, supervisor, or team leader to determine whether or not a formal corrective action needs to be enacted. When considering whether or not a formal corrective action should be enacted, one or more of the following issues should be considered.

1. Estimated potential risk and/or liability resulting from the nonconformity. Suggested tools: Process of product failure mode and effect analysis.

2. Cost of solution, that is, the internal and external costs (if available) associated with the creation of a corrective action team.

3. Whether or not the problem is a recurrent one, nature and frequency of the recurrence, and potential impact on the internal or external cost of the recurrence. Suggested tool and/or available data: Pareto analysis, nonconformity database.

If any or all of these items suggest that a formal corrective action is required, proceed further.

4.14.2 Corrective Action

The same corrective action process will be applied irrespective of the nature of the corrective action, however, the person or function responsible for the corrective action will vary accordingly and may involve one or more persons.

Once it is determined that the corrective action process must be implemented, records of all activities relating to follow-up activities, meetings, and resolution of the issue must be maintained by a designated individual who will be responsible for bringing the corrective action to closure. At a minimum, a corrective action form (see Figures 5.5 and 5.6) must be maintained for each case. Supporting documents such as engineering review (when required), minutes of meetings, any correspondence, and data, such as laboratory analysis or other necessary documents, can be added to the file as required.

When the recommended solution requires changes in a process and/or procedure, the person responsible for the process and/or procedure is required to implement, within a mutually agreed-upon time period, the necessary changes, ensure that changes are duly recorded (see Document Control), determine whether or not additional training will be required, and inform the person(s) in charge of internal audits. On the assumption that the process is still active, the effectiveness of the corrective action will be monitored during subsequent internal audits. Audit reports are submitted to management for quarterly reviews. The duration of this monitoring is

Figure 5.4. Sample procedure written to address paragraph 4.14.

left to the discretion of the audit manager. If objective evidence indicates that the corrective action is ineffective, the corrective process may be repeated if the risks associated with the problems are at least equal to prior assessments.

4.14.3 Preventive Action

XYZ Inc. relies on several sources of information (customer feedback, field reports, sales/marketing reports, audit reports, employee suggestions to analyze and eliminate, whenever economically feasible, potential causes of nonconformities. This would include improvements in safety or any other processes directly related to activities specified in this quality system. The preventive action process follows the same guidelines as those found in the corrective action guidelines.

Cross-references: Audit reports, management quarterly reviews, and corrective and preventive action files.

(Note: The use of cross-referencing is encouraged. This cross-reference cites audit reports, management reviews, and corrective and preventive actions.)

Figure 5.4. *(continued)*

Corrective/Preventive Action Form (Select one)

Corrective/Preventive action number: _____   Date: _____
Originator (internal or external): _____
Description of the nonconformance:

_____
_____

Result of investigation (use additional pages as required):

_____
_____

Process change: Yes   No   (circle one)
If yes, which process(es): _____
Person or team responsible to implement process change:

_____

Investigating team/departments:

_____

Closure date: _____ by: _____
Copies sent to:

Figure 5.5. Sample blank corrective action form used for internal audits.

Corrective/Preventive Action Form (select one)

Corrective ✔/Preventive action number: IQA 09 Date: February 13, 1995
Originator (internal or external): Internal audit team (lead: John Doe)

Description of the nonconformance: While auditing purchasing, the
audit team discovered that a critical part (cite part and
purchase order number) was ordered from an unapproved supplier (cite supplier). This is contrary to current
purchasing procedure (cite particular paragraph).

Result of investigation (use additional pages as required): After review with
the purchasing manager, it was discovered that the current (approved) supplier was not able to deliver the part in time hence
the selection of a second supplier. The supplier did satisfy our
minimum requirements as specified in our questionnaire and was
provisionally approved, but records of the approval were not
logged in.

Process change: Yes   No ✔ (check one)
If Yes, which process(es): _____
Person or team responsible to implement process change: The purchasing manager will ensure that the supplier's name is entered in the provisional list of approved suppliers. Corrective action will be
closed by February 28, 1995.
Investigating team/departments: Internal quality audit team and manager of purchasing department.

Closure date: Next audit (December 15, 1995) by: John Doe
Copies sent to: Purchasing manager

Figure 5.6. Completed sample corrective action form used for internal audits.

4.6   Purchasing
4.6.1   General

The following procedure ensures that purchased product conforms to XYZ Inc. specified requirements and/or government standards.

4.6.2   Evaluation of Subcontractors

XYZ Inc. has conducted business with numerous subcontractors and suppliers. Suppliers and subcontractors are evaluated based on their technical competence, ability to deliver a job on time, and price competitiveness. The nature, extent, and type of control exercised by XYZ Inc. on its suppliers and/or subcontractors naturally depends on the type of product purchased and its impact on the quality of the final product.

Approval Process

New suppliers or subcontractors are placed on a provisional approval list for a period of one or more months depending on the importance of the order. The length of the probation period is decided by the purchasing manager, salesperson, or supervisor (or all three) in charge of the product and is effective only after the first purchase is made. At the end of the probation period, the supplier may then be included in the list of approved suppliers depending on his performance.

All other suppliers with which XYZ Inc. has done business for more than one year prior to achieving ISO 9002 certification were automatically included on the list of approved suppliers, but were informed that they were subject to the evaluation rules.

Type of Suppliers

XYZ Inc. has identified two types of approved suppliers; critical and noncritical. Critical suppliers, identified by the letter C in the purchasing database, are evaluated by the manager in charge of the product based on their technical ability to meet specified requirements and on-time delivery. On occasion, site visits may be required to acquire additional information.

Noncritical suppliers, which would also include suppliers of office supplies and/or support services such as certain maintenance services and third-party calibration services, are not evaluated. They may be dropped for a variety of reasons including price and/or performance.

Supplier Retention/Evaluation

Technical ability is periodically assessed by the product engineer by randomly sampling parts to verify conformance to requirement. Nonconformities are identified by supplier in the nonconformity data base. Copies of the nonconformity form are faxed to the suppliers and/or subcontractors for review, comment, and reply. Replies are required within 48 hours: exceptions to this rule are left to the discretion of the manager responsible for the disposition of the nonconformity. It is the responsibility of the quality manager or supervisor to review the nonconformity database at least once a quarter and decide, based on objective evidence, whether or not a critical supplier

Figure 5.7. Sample purchasing procedure (4.6).

should be dropped from the list of approved suppliers. Recommendations for dropping a supplier must be formally presented during XYZ Inc. weekly management meetings. A majority vote is all that is required for dropping a supplier.

4.6.3   Purchasing Data

Purchase orders contain all the pertinent data necessary to ensure that the correct item and/or service is specified. When required, the type, class, and grade of a product or revision of a drawing, code, or specification are clearly specified.

When called for, additional information such as inspection requirements, reference to national or international standards, or other technical requirements are also clearly stated on the purchase document.

Purchase orders over $800 require review and approval by the purchasing manager.

4.6.4   Verification of Purchased Product

XYZ Inc. does not verify purchased product at the subcontractor's or supplier's premises. Hence this requirement is not applicable to XYZ Inc.

6.6.4.2 Customer Verification of Subcontracted Product

Presently, none of XYZ Inc.'s customers require that product shall be evaluated at the subcontractor's premises or XYZ Inc.'s premises. Should this requirement be requested by any of our customers, then XYZ Inc. will implement the appropriate verification procedure.

Figure 5.7. *(continued)*

pH of 4.0. Calibrate your pH meter at 4.0 and 8.0, for example. This will allow you to determine whether or not your instrument is accurate over a specified range of measurements and not at just one point. Of course, if all of your measurements are to be made around 4.0, the linearity of the instrument may be irrelevant. The same principle applies to scales.

Finally, remember that paragraph 4.11 requires you to assess the accuracy and precision of your instrument. Accuracy and precision are occasionally confused with calibration.

> The accuracy of an instrument is the extent to which the average of a long series of repeat measurements made by the instrument on a single unit of product differs from the true value. This difference is usually due to a systematic error in the measurement process. In this case, the instrument is said to be out of calibra-

tion. The precision of an instrument is the extent towhich the instrument repeats its results when making repeat measurements on the same unit of product. The scatter of these measurements may be designated as sigma (Σ), meaning the standard deviation of measurement error. The lower the value of sigma (Σ) the more "precise" is the instrument.[3]

Determining the accuracy, particularly the precision, of each instrument is costly if you have many instruments. You will need to take repeated measures of at least two (but preferably more) of the same part or sample and conduct what is known as a repeatability and reproducibility study (see gauge R&R study in Part II). Fortunately, you may not have to determine the precision of all your instruments (calibration may be all that you need). It may be that the nature of your measurements does not require you to assess precision, or it could be that the nature of your business is such (service sector) that you do not use instruments to measure variables.

Table 5.1 is a simple way to identify all equipment that will require calibration. If you have a computer, the table can easily be

Table 5.1. Sample table for equipment calibration due date.

Equipment	Location/ I.D. No.	Frequency	Next Due Date
pH meter (2)	Laboratory 101203 and 101204	Daily	N/A
Micrometers (6)	Work station: 5–8 00531, 00643, 00234, 00448, 00323, 00832	Monthly or more frequently if mishandled.	5th of every month
Scales (3)	Laboratory 101, 102, 103	Daily	N/A
List other equipment as required.			

included in a database. Specialized software packages are available to keep track of equipment calibration location and due date.

Statistical Techniques (4.20)

This paragraph is often misunderstood. It requires that you identify the "need for statistical techniques," which will help you determine whether or not your processes are statistically capable (see Part II for further discussion). Once you have determined which statistical techniques you will be using, you must develop a procedure to "control the application of the identified statistical technique." In other words, you must ensure that the technique is correctly applied.

The paragraph does not specify the use of statistical techniques. In fact, it could be that the nature of your processes or products are not conducive to statistical analysis, in which case you may not be able to make effective use of statistical techniques.

The most common SPC technique that could be used to satisfy the requirements of paragraph 4.20 is control charts (also know as Shewhart charts). This technique, made popular by Dr. Shewhart in the 1920s, allows you to determine if your processes are statistically capable. Although the technique of control charts has found many applications in the manufacturing and service world, it is not suitable for all business environments. Control charts allow you to determine whether or not you are capable of producing certain product characteristics within limits. If you are in the business of producing low-volume customized products, or if tolerances are nonexistent or are not quantified but rather qualified, it will be difficult, if not impossible, to implement SPC (see chapter 17 for examples).

Many techniques—statistical and others—can be used with several of the ISO 9001, ISO 9002, or ISO 9003 paragraphs. Table 5.2 identifies techniques that could be used with certain paragraphs. A brief definition for most of these techniques is provided in Part II.

Conclusions

The development of a quality assurance system designed to comply with the ISO 9000 series of standards need not be a complex task. Small businesses cannot afford to appoint an army of individuals to plan and develop a quality assurance system. The creation of an ISO

Table 5.2. Relationship between a few statistical techniques and ISO 9001 paragraphs.

Sample of Possible Techniques	Potential ISO 9001 Applications
Acceptance sampling	4.10.2
Analysis of variance	4.11 and 4.14, 4.20
Brainstorming	4.13, 4.14
Cause-and-effect diagram (see also Pareto)	4.13, 4.14, 4.17
Design of experiment	4.4, 4.14
Failure mode and effect analysis (process and product)	4.4, 4.14
Flow diagram	4.9a and most other paragraphs where a process or procedure may have to be described
Histogram	4.6, 4.9, 4.10, 4.20, and many others
Pareto	4.6, 4.13
SPC Other techniques: Regression analysis, factor analysis	4.9d, 4.14.2, 4.14.3, 4.20 4.4, 4.14

9000 implementation team consisting of five to six individuals, although feasible for medium-size businesses, may not be practical for small businesses. Indeed, a team of five to six individuals could represent as much as 30 percent (assuming 20 employees) of the staff of a small business (equivalent to as many as 300 individuals for a company of 1000). For most small businesses, where resources are often stretched to the limit, allocating 30 percent of the workforce to ISO 9000 implementation efforts is an impossible task. Yet, the effort may only need to be short term. Moreover, the more people who are involved, the less time each individual would have to allocate. This advice will also help you better organize the internal audit process, the subject of the next chapter.

Notes

1. In an article entitled "Errors Renew the Call for Doctor Review," Deborah Sharp cites examples of a man who had the wrong foot amputated, a woman who had the wrong breast removed, and a person who died of an overdose of a highly toxic cancer drug. *USA TODAY*, 27 March 1995, p. 3.

2. The company had installed so-called scrubbers to remove sulphur and thus take care of the problem. The process of producing ammonium nitrate is apparently robust enough to accept a broad range of raw material quality and still produce a quality product for farmers.

3. J. M. Juran and F. M. Gryna Jr., *Quality Planning and Analysis*, 4th ed. (New York: McGraw-Hill, 1980), 390.

6 How to Facilitate an Internal Audit

The Need for Internal Audit[1]

The conduct of internal audits is clearly specified by paragraph 4.17 of ISO 9001, ISO 9002, and ISO 9003. Moreover, paragraph 4.1.2.2, Resources, specifies that, "The supplier shall identify resource requirements and provide adequate training, including the assignment of trained personnel (see 4.18), for management, performance of work, and verification activities including internal quality audits." To ensure compliance with paragraphs 4.17 and 4.1.2.2, many companies enroll several of their employees into one of the many five-day lead assessor courses currently offered by a few officially approved consulting or training agencies. Some large companies even invite consulting agencies for in-house two- to five-day auditor training for as many as 20 to 60 of their employees. Obviously, this practice is not likely to be cost-effective for small businesses.

A Word of Caution Regarding Lead Assessor Training

There seems to be some confusion and occasionally some unrealistic expectations as to what these five-day lead assessor courses provide. Lead assessor courses are designed for individuals who want to become professional auditors. Ever since their first appearance in the United States in 1990, these courses have attracted thousands of individuals who think that if they learn how to audit, they will automatically learn how to implement a quality assurance system that would conform to one of the ISO 9000 standards. Unfortunately, this is not true; the two skills are not necessarily related.

Yet another belief is that a company must have internal auditors trained as lead assessors. Again, that is not required by the standards, although many training agencies would like you to believe otherwise. Finally, people seem to think that if they take the course, they automatically will be qualified for the glorified position of ISO 9000 auditor. That is also not true. Moreover, as the market becomes increasingly flooded with auditors, more and more people are rapidly realizing that, given the long hours and the substantial amount of travelling, being an ISO 9000 auditor is no longer as financially rewarding as it was once perceived to be.

To become an ISO 9000–certified auditor, you must do more than just attend a course. You must also pass a two-hour exam (more than 75 percent of those taking the exam pass it). Just passing the exam does not automatically qualify you as a certified auditor. This is where the confusion starts. In order to be considered a potential ISO 9000 auditor, you must have four years of related experience (two in quality), and you must also participate in four audits for a total of at least 20 days. These audits must be led by a certified lead auditor. Having conducted the required number of audits, you may then apply (for a fee of $300 in the United States) to the national accreditation body (Registrar Accreditation Board in the United States) for official recognition and eventual certification. If you are accepted, your name will be included in an official register. Then, and only then, are you considered a certified ISO 9000 auditor.

Internal Audits

Internal quality audits are one of the few companywide activities required by paragraph 4.17 of ISO 9001, ISO 9002, and ISO 9003. The paragraph requires a company to assess the effectiveness and continued feasibility of its quality assurance system. Internal audits should be conducted as soon as the documented quality assurance system is in place. One need not wait until the system is fully documented to conduct the first audit. In fact, the audit team can conduct a couple of audits as the system is being implemented. There are several advantages for doing so. First, it allows both parties—auditors and auditees—to interpret, question, evaluate, and analyze firsthand the everyday practical issues surrounding the standard. Also, it allows the audit team to monitor the implementation progress of each department. Valuable lessons can be learned on how a particular department addressed a set of requirements. Finally, the auditors get to practice their auditing skills.

It has been my experience that during the early stages of internal auditing, most audit teams—having intimate knowledge of the processes and the weaknesses of the working system—tend to focus on uncovering as many nonconformances as possible. In some cases, some of the nonconformances are tangentially related to ISO 9000, in other cases they tend to be of the nit-picking, "I got you" nature. Internal audits that merely focus on the policing aspect of auditing quickly lose their credibility and thus effectiveness. Conducted properly, however, first-party (internal) audits provide an excellent opportunity to verify whether or not the documented system is indeed implemented at all levels.

Internal audits should be

- Procedural
- Planned and documented to determine the effectiveness of the quality system
- Scheduled according to the status and importance of the activity

The last item simply means that you have the option to audit each department as frequently as you wish. For example, you may wish to audit all affected departments twice a year, or you may choose to audit your laboratory every quarter and the purchasing department once a year. Although the frequency of audits is left to the supplier's discretion, it is not reasonable to suggest (as I once read in a quality manual) that "internal audits will be conducted when deemed necessary." Most companies plan internal audits at least twice a year.

In addition, audit findings shall be documented and brought to the attention of the appropriate manager(s), who shall take "timely corrective action."

When addressing internal quality audits, it is important to remember Shewhart's plan, do, check, act cycle (PDCA). The internal audit team must not only schedule the audit (plan), it must also conduct the audit (do), verify that the documented system matches the implemented system (check), and most importantly, management must act upon all nonconformances in a timely fashion (act). An audit status report with many "no reply" comments can indicate that management is not taking the internal audit process very seriously (see the section on closure).

Familiarity with the Standard

No amount of preparation will help you if you are not familiar with the content of the appropriate ISO 9000 standard. Unfortunately, in-depth knowledge of the standard can only be acquired through repeated readings and application of the standard. Consequently, do not be surprised or frustrated if, during your first couple of internal audits, you feel somewhat uneasy, not sure of what to ask or look for. This is a natural process. This is why it is important, in the early stages, to have a well-prepared audit plan and a checklist of questions (just in case you don't know what to ask for). During the first couple of audits, I recommend that two or three internal auditors audit the same department. This allows each member of the audit team to think of the next question while a fellow team member is pursuing a line of questioning. Be careful not to rapidly ask too many questions simultaneously at the auditee. Take turns and be patient. Finally, do not feel compelled to search until you have found what you consider to be an appropriate quota of nonconformances. In the majority of cases you should not have to search too long before nonconformances are uncovered or volunteered by the auditee.

Internal audit teams conducting preassessment audits may be faced with yet another difficulty—the absence of a fully documented quality assurance system. Nonetheless, although it might be difficult to develop a relevant checklist without the help of a quality manual or other pertinent documents, such checklists can nonetheless be written. When auditing an undocumented system, auditors are faced with the additional challenge of literally discovering/understanding the system as they simultaneously audit it! When faced with such a situation, I suggest that a consultant might be the most efficient way to assess ISO 9000 readiness.

Preparation

Preparing for an internal audit usually does not require as much time as preparing for a third-party (independent/external) audit. This is due to the fact that even though the internal auditors do not audit their own department, they nonetheless have (or should have) a more in-depth understanding of their company than any external third-party auditor. Nonetheless, some preparation will be required, particularly in the early stages. The following activities are recommended.

• Ensure that the people you will be auditing are well aware of the various ISO 9000 requirements. I have participated in some internal audits where the auditee(s) had never seen the ISO 9000 standards. It is difficult to comprehend how an organization could attempt to implement an ISO 9000 quality assurance system—and conduct internal audits—without informing the affected departments as to what is required. One easy and *partly* effective way to do so is to, at a minimum, distribute copies of the standard to all concerned parties. I emphasize partly because the standard still needs to be interpreted and applied to the company's needs. See Sample 2 on page 118 for suggestions on how to address these issues.

• Define the *purpose* and *scope* of your audit (see Sample 3 on page 119). The scope should define what will be audited and to what standard or paragraph within a standard.

• Estimate how much resources (time and staffpower) will be required. The size of the audit team will naturally vary with the size of the organization. Some companies make the mistake of assigning the internal audit function to only one person. Auditing is a demanding, if not tedious, activity, so it is imperative to share the audit responsibilities with more than one person. Failure to do so will quickly lead to burnout. Moreover, the internal audit process is much too important to trust to only one person.

Many companies train anywhere from 2 to 20 people to become internal ISO 9000 auditors. There is really no right number or scientific formula that one can apply to determine the correct number of internal auditors, except to say that it must be greater than one. Medium-size companies should have at least two to six individuals in charge of audits (one or more lead auditor[s] and one to five auditors).

• Schedule the time and day of the audit. Ensure that there are no scheduling conflicts with the auditee(s). See Samples 1 and 2 on pages 117 and 118).

• Decide on which audit trail method(s) the team will adopt. A few options are available. You could

1. Follow the product downstream from purchasing/marketing to receiving inspection *down* to shipping.

2. Reverse the process and move upstream.

3. Plan a particular audit trail that would combine upstream and downstream auditing.

4. Assign appropriate (ISO 9000) paragraphs to team members and periodically meet to consult and share notes.

5. Develop your own style, which might include a combination of all of the above options.

• For the first few audits, you may want to develop a checklist, which will help remind you what questions to ask. What documents will you want to see? (Note and caveat: This is particularly important during your first two or three audits. Please remember that the checklist is *not* a substitute for the audit, nor is it a simple rephrasing of the ISO 9000 standards. Some auditors, even professional third-party auditors, seem to be totally enamored with their checklist, never deviating from its contents. The checklist is nothing more than a reminder of what needs to be done).

• Establish a list of all relevant documents that will be needed during your audit. Familiarize yourself with the contents of the written documents. Review the appropriate sections of the quality manual, read process documentation, establish which records are supposed to be collected, decide what measurements are supposed to be made, and so on. As you read these documents, do not hesitate to write comments and mark paragraphs (assuming you have copies and not the originals). This will allow you to estimate how much time your interviews will take. It will also help you determine what questions you will need to ask.

• If you are not familiar with the process, a schematic of the process(es) would be helpful. If none is available, have someone explain the flow to you. This will help you formulate specific questions during the audit.

Human Relations Skills

Any auditor must learn to develop some human relations skills. The purpose of the audit is, in part, to ensure that the documented system matches the actual (working) system. This exercise does not imply that an auditor must find as many nonconformances as possible or that he/she must audit until at least one or more nonconformance(s) is/are found. One of the main functions of the auditor is to assist in the continued application/implementation and improvement of the quality assurance system. To achieve that goal, the auditor must learn to listen and get input from people on how the system can be improved. As Nancy W. Girvin explains, "it is people we audit (not the requirements), people who get our report (not the findings), and people who make effective corrective action happen (not the audit)."[2]

Rather than perceiving the internal auditor as a friend, some persons unfortunately tend to perceive the auditor as

- A stranger who should not be trusted
- Someone whom he/she does not really want to talk to, but has to
- Someone who wastes precious time
- Someone a bit too curious
- Someone who is looking for a crack in the system and usually finds it

In order to avoid mistrust and doubt, the auditor should clearly state the purpose of the audit. This step is equally important for internal audits. If the system is ineffective, then recommendations must be sought on how to improve the system rather than blindly enforcing it. Punitive actions and negative and particularly destructive criticism or sarcasm must be avoided and are counterproductive. Such actions can only lead to catastrophic results.

Throughout any audit, a good auditor

- Carefully and attentively listens
- Demonstrates a genuine interest
- Never judges or criticizes
- Is patient
- Neither approves nor disapproves
- Does not prepare the next question while listening to an answer
- Should never be vindictive, nor suspicious, but rather trustworthy
- Maintains eye contact

Successful Interviews

Most audits (internal or third-party) involve interviewing quite a few people. Since an interview is essentially a method of collecting information, steps must be taken to ensure that pertinent information is being gathered.

There are several factors involved in conducting interviews. The following guidelines, based on third-party auditors, may also be practiced by first-party auditors, although probably with less rigor since the internal auditors are likely to know all of their coworkers.

Assuming that each member of the internal audit team is a willing participant, the success of your internal audits will generally depend on

- The amount of preparation and organization of the audit team
- The degree of familiarity with the standard and the company's quality system
- The human relations skills of each member

- The type of reporting
- The success rate of your closures

Conducting the Interview

One of the advantages of internal audits is that, unlike third-party audits, they do not have to be completed within two to five days. Internal audits can be conducted anytime, and they do not have to last more than three to four hours. Still, since you will be interviewing several people, it is impossible to remember who said what when. Hence, it is good practice to always carry along a small notebook whenever touring a plant or interviewing people. You may also want to include time of day and the name of the person being interviewed (a technique used by some third-party auditors). If people find it difficult to talk to you while you write notes, try either to limit your notetaking to key words or simply stop writing altogether.

Whether you take complete or partial notes, you should always allow 10 to 15 minutes at the end of each interview to prepare your own summary of what has been said. Such in-between-interview pauses are extremely valuable, particularly if you like to audit for one or two consecutive days. These pauses

1. Allow you to collect your thoughts and summarize what has been said, permitting you to modify or otherwise prepare for your next interview.

2. Provide you with a needed rest period between interviews. Such pauses are important if you want to remain an effective listener for the duration of the interview/audit. Naturally, you could avoid this problem by simply scheduling your internal audits over several mornings. Remember that unlike third-party audits, you are not required to complete your internal audits within a couple of days. You can take as long as you want.

Formulating Questions

A good question is a question that

- Is clear and complete and facilitates the auditee's response
- Does not accuse or attack
- Does not influence and allows the auditee to freely answer

Do not forget that the purpose of any audit is to collect facts; that is why questions must

- Stimulate thoughtfulness
- Channel information
- Provoke a reaction
- Provide explanations
- Explore, clarify, verify, and illustrate

The quality audit should be designed to collect *facts* and not vague statements; precision is of the essence. Answers such as "Many," "A few," and "Quite a bit" should prompt the auditor to ask, "How much?" "Always," "Often," and "Generally" should prompt "When?" Statements such as "Generally," "In principle," and "In theory" should prompt "And in particular," "And in reality," and "And in practice." Questions should always avoid referring to opinions, feelings, or vague concepts.

Types of Questions
There are basically two types of questions: open-ended questions and closed questions. Closed questions are very limiting in that they are conducive to laconic answers: yes, no, five, and so on. Although these questions lead to very precise answers, they tend to discourage any dialogue.

Open-ended questions or requests allow for greater flexibility. Examples of open-ended questions include

"How do you control bath temperature?"
"Why do you have this particular control?"
"Tell me more about your calibration procedure."
"Could you please explain your incoming material inspection procedure?"

Some questions are designed to obtain clarification. Examples include

"What do you mean when you say 'it's always the same thing'?"
"Could you give me an example of . . . ?"

Auditors should monitor themselves to avoid expressing opinions or asking false questions, which really are not questions but rather opinions. Some examples are

"Don't you think that is a lot of rejects (rework, scrap)?"

"Isn't that a high external cost?"

"Don't you think management is dragging its feet?"

Repetition and Silence

It is often very helpful to repeat the answer(s) you have just heard to confirm with the auditee your understanding. This mirror effect can be very helpful. Examples of lead-ins for such statements follows.

"To summarize,...

"If I understand what you just said,..."

"Therefore, as far as you are concerned,..."

"It is therefore your opinion that..."

It is generally believed that during an interview, 20 to 30 percent of the time should be taken by the auditor and the balance should be granted to the auditee. In order to respect such a ratio, the auditor should learn to remain

- Silent, but attentive and interested

- Silent, but observing and listening

- Silent but taking notes

The auditor should always avoid interrupting the auditee or talking at the same time.

How to Ask Questions

1. Avoid asking questions too rapidly. Do not rush through your interview.

2. Avoid asking more than one question at a time.

3. Avoid asking lengthy questions.

Since questions can be a very effective tool to acquire information they must be carefully stated. Do not forget that from the point of view of the auditee, your questions will generally be perceived as a form of intrusion. Every time you ask a question, you in some way impose your frame of reference within which the auditee must try to answer to the best of his/her ability. See Table 6.1 for suggestions on how to handle difficult interviews.

When terminating an interview, the interviewer should give the respondent the opportunity to add anything else that he or she thinks is significant.

What Is a Nonconformance?

A nonconformance is either a failure to address a specific requirement of ISO 9001, ISO 9002, or ISO 9003, or a failure to perform a task or set of tasks specified in the quality assurance system (for example, the quality manual and supporting procedures.) To some auditors, the slightest deviation from a procedure—such as a missing signature, for example—is immediately considered a failure of the system. To others, a pattern of (unjustified or undocumented) deviations would have to be uncovered (that is, several signatures would have to be missing) for the system to be judged inadequate.

When examining nonconformities, the auditor must consider not only the frequency of occurrence, but also the severity of the nonconformity. Irrespective of their nature, *all* nonconformities should be noted and discussed during the closure meeting, for they indicate that an element of the system may need to be adjusted. Perhaps the audited procedure is no longer applicable and needs to be updated or perhaps more operator training is required. (see problem-solving technique discussions in Part II).

If you remember that the purpose of an internal audit is to constantly find ways to improve a system and not to find failures within a system, your internal audits will be a valuable tool.

Table 6.1. Suggestions for difficult interviews.

Respondent Behavior	Interviewer Action
1. Appears to guess at answers rather than admit ignorance.	1. After the interview, cross-check answers that are suspect.
2. Attempts to tell the interviewer what he or she presumably wants to hear instead of the correct facts.	2. Avoid putting questions in a form that implies the answers. Cross-check answers that are suspect.
3. Gives the interviewer a great deal of irrelevant information or tells stories.	3. In friendly but persistent fashion, bring the discussion back into desired channel.
4. Stops talking if the interviewer takes notes.	4. Put the notebook away.
5. Attempts to rush through the interview.	5. Suggest coming back later.
6. Expresses satisfaction with the way things are done now and wants no change.	6. Encourage respondent to elaborate on present situation and its virtues.
7. Shows obvious resentment of the interviewer, answers questions guardedly, or appears to be withholding data.	7. Try to get the respondent to talk about something that interests him or her.
8. Sabotages the interview by noncooperation.	8. Ask the respondent if you can get the information from someone else.
9. Gripes about the job, the pay, associates, supervisors, or the unfair treatment he or she receives.	9. Be sympathetic and listen for clues. Then suggest how those gripes can be of help to the company.
10. Acts as eager beaver, is enthusiastic about new ideas, gadgets, techniques.	10. Listen for desired facts and valuable leads.

Reporting

Once you have completed the audit, you should conduct a brief exit interview, which is followed by a brief formal audit report. During the exit interview you will need to present and, if need be, discuss your preliminary findings. As an internal auditor, your objective is to ensure that your findings are as concrete as possible. You should be able to state

- The nature of the nonconformance.

- Where the nonconformance occurred (department, assembly line, person interviewed).

- The nature of the nonconformance, that is, whether it is a written or verbal evidence.

- When the nonconformance occurred (date, some even include the time).

- Which ISO 9000 paragraph applies. This apparently trite observation is worth stating because some auditors tend to forget that they are auditing to an ISO 9000 standard.

- Which section of the company quality manual or other tiers apply.

During your presentation and/or final report, you should avoid including long lists of identical or nearly identical nonconformances. Rather, you should attempt to cluster similar deficiencies as elements of one global finding. There are a couple of advantages in doing so. First of all, the reporting of cluster findings demonstrates that the auditor has a good command of the auditing process, and more importantly, that the overall system has been evaluated. Secondly, cluster findings are more likely to be accepted simply because, unlike the old-fashioned nitpicking deficiencies, they are perceived to be more reasonable. I should warn, however, that what is considered nitpicking in one industry (for example, manufacture of foam used for packaging) might be considered of critical importance in another (for example, pharmaceutical or aerospace industries).

If everyone agrees with the nonconformances, the next step is to propose a schedule as to when and how the nonconformances will be resolved.

Closure

This follow-up activity is occasionally ignored by the department responsible for addressing the corrective actions. Closure can not be achieved until corrective actions are implemented (see Sample 5 on page 122).

How to Be Ready for an Audit

Whenever an organization or department is about to be audited, a certain amount of preparation may need to take place; however, you should not have to prepare for an audit since that implies that you behave and operate one way during the audit and another way after the audit! The following guidelines are probably better suited for third-party audits.

1. Make sure everyone knows well in advance when the audit will take place. (Note: Some internal auditors prefer to conduct their audits unannounced, perhaps hoping to catch the "villains" in a flagrant act of nonconformance. Although you could conduct your internal audits unannounced, the idea of catching anyone is really counter-productive and can very well lead to some animosity between employees.)

2. Be relaxed.

3. It is often a good idea to rehearse an audit (hence the value of internal audits). In most cases, the pre-audit should be conducted by an outside (independent) source. This will guarantee objectivity. One does not rehearse in the hope of better fooling the auditor (although this is often the intent). Rather, rehearsing allows the auditee to focus on the eventual audit (see next point).

4. When the auditors arrive, do not try to hide your weaknesses. Doing so will encourage a good auditor to be even more inquisitive. On the other hand, for third-party audits, do not volunteer information not requested by the auditor. This can be achieved by

keeping your answers short and to the point. Make sure you have all pertinent documentation ready for the auditors' inspection.

Samples

The examples on the following pages cover

- Advance notice of upcoming audits (Sample 1)
- How to inform auditee of intended audit (Sample 2)
- Audit report format (Sample 3)
- Audit evaluation questionnaire (Sample 4)
- Audit finding response form (Sample 5)
- Audit status report (Sample 6)

These samples should provide the reader with enough guidelines on how to address the ISO 9000 internal quality audit clause. Caveats and comments are added in italics.

Sample 1

It is a good idea to offer advance warning as to when each department will be audited.

Distribution:

Name	Department
Steve Mickey	Product Engineering
Robert Hall	Metrology
Allan Moor	Purchasing
Joyce Hornbeck	Quality Assurance
Bruce Middleton	Training
Jack Finn	Manufacturing
Lou Prout	Manufacturing Engineer
Charles Hilde	Packaging/Shipping
Ernest Ross	Laboratory
Linda Kazascky	Marketing
Tom Jurge	R&D
Curt Williams	Maintenance
Bill Andrews	Human Resources
Jim Jurgens	Technical Services

To: Distribution   October 13, 1995

Re: 1996 Audit Schedule   From: Jim Lamprecht

This tentative schedule is intended to give managers and supervisors advance notice of audits scheduled in their areas. You will be notified approximately four weeks prior to the audit. The size of the audit team will depend on the scope and department being audited, but will not exceed two auditors.

Month	*Audit type–scope*	*Department*
January	Document requirement	Training
January	Lab doc. control/procedures	Laboratory
February	Calibration procedure and training	Metrology
March	Procedure-change control plus work instructions	Production control
March	Traceability	Quality assurance production
April	Sample analysis procedures	Laboratory
April	Packaging/shipping procedures	Shipping
April	Documentation, vendor evaluation	Purchasing

Sample 2
This memo informs the auditee of the upcoming audit.

To: Bruce Hightower   December 18, 1995
       Human Resources

From: Jim Lamprecht

Re: Training documentation requirements as per paragraph 4.18 of
ISO 9001

I will be conducting an audit of your department on January 17,
1996. The audit will focus on the current documentation system
and should not last more than 45 minutes. The reference for the
audit will be paragraph 4.18 of ISO 9001, which reads as follows:

> **4.18 Training**
> The supplier shall establish and maintain docu-
> mented procedures for identifying training needs
> and provide for the training of all personnel per-
> forming activities affecting quality. Personnel per-
> forming specific assigned tasks shall be qualified on
> the basis of appropriate education, training, and/or
> experience, as required. Appropriate records of
> training shall be maintained (see 4.16). (*Note: Para-
> graph 4.16 should also be included for cross-reference.*)

I will forward a schedule by January 10, 1996, along with a tentative
schedule for the audit. If this schedule is not suitable, please feel
free to contact me at X-5555.

                                    Jim Lamprecht
                                    Lead Internal Auditor

cc: Appropriate managers

Sample 3

This is an example of how you might want to format your audit report findings.

To: Manager
From: Auditor or audit team
Re: Audit #95-05: Sampling Procedure Book

Purpose

The purpose of the audit is to review all of the sampling procedures books as to completeness and up-to-date status (paragraph 4.5.1 and 4.5.2, Document and Data Control of ISO 9001) of inspection procedures.

Scope

All 52 sampling procedure books will be reviewed according to SP-A-1, III.E.1.

Procedure

All books found were audited by the same method. The master index date was checked; then five randomly selected standard procedures were checked for verified appropriate revisions.

Observations

- Sampling procedures number 18, 22, and 37 were not found.
- 22 percent of all sampling procedure books had the wrong master index sheet *(may want to list)*.
- 12 percent of the standard procedures had outdated revision numbers *(may want to list)*.
- 30 percent of the standard procedures had numerous uncontrolled handwritten notes *(may want to list)*.

Recommendations

1. Update standard procedures having handwritten notes as well as the master index sheet.
2. Your suggestion to computerize (via word processing) the SP book should be implemented as soon as possible. It could certainly reduce your paperwork. However, how will you inform marketing of all your updates? As you know, we are required to inform some of our clients of any sampling and testing updates.

Congratulations on the excellent job of maintaining the SP books. The number of nonconformances has been significantly reduced from our last audit #94-11.

Sample 4

It is always a good idea to ask the people you audit to critique the audit process. This sample illustrates how you might want to evaluate the effectiveness of your audit. You might want to adapt or otherwise modify the questionnaire to best suit your needs.

Quality Audit Program Evaluation
It would be helpful if you would add any constructive comments or observations concerning your experience as an auditee. You do not need to identify yourself by name. Please indicate your position.
_____ Supervisor   _____ Department head _____ Manager   _____ Operator Department _____
Comments:

Sample 4 *(continued)*
Please evaluate the following questions using the five-point scale:
1 = Strongly disagree, 2 = Disagree, 3 = No opinion, 4 = Agree,
5 =Strongly agree.

Questions	1	2	3	4	5
1. The audit was a fair appraisal of my operation.					
2. Interference with operations was at a minimum.					
3. The audit did not take long.					
4. I was notified prior to the audit and agreed to the time.					
5. The auditor was objective, fair, and listened to my opinions.					
6. The auditor only reported discrepancies that were observed and confirmed by me.					
7. Disagreements were resolved equitably.					
8. The auditor was knowledgeable and qualified.					
9. The auditor(s) was/were prepared and proceeded in an organized and efficient manner.					
10. The auditor was considerate of our time constraints and was flexible.					
11. The audit was comprehensive and thorough.					
12. Minor deficiencies were clustered into a global finding.					
13. The auditor clearly distinguished factual (objective) evidence from hearsay.					
14. I was kept informed of the audit observations during the audit.					
15. I was the first to know the audit results in my area of responsibility.					
16. Corrective actions will be implemented.					
17. The audit report did not embarrass me or make me feel defensive.					
18. The audit helped me to more effectively control quality and reduce costs.					
19. The audit helped me to better perform my job.					
20. I think the audit program is helpful and is a worthwhile effort.					
Average					

Sample 5

Audit Finding Response Form
Audit # 95-02   Finding # 1   Date: May 18, 1995
Audit Title: Document control/Change control as per ISO 9001 § 4.5.1 and 4.5.2.
Finding: Sampling procedures Lab 01-D-132 and Lab 12-F-13 were not up to date.
Cause of the problem:
Action(s) to be taken to correct and prevent recurrence:
By whom and when will corrective action be implemented?
Prepared by:_____ Date _____
(For internal lead auditor only) Follow-up audit required: No_____ Yes_____ By when?_____ Audit finding closed? Yes_____ No_____ Reason: _____

Sample 6

Finding Status Report			
Definitions			
Open findings:	Findings reported on audits		
In-process findings:	Findings that are not yet due or not yet closed		
Overdue findings:	Findings that are more than 30 days overdue		
	Open findings 11		
	In-process findings 09		
	Overdue findings 02		
	Total 22		

Some auditors summarize their status report by department as follows:

Department	Open	In-process	Overdue
Purchasing	2		
Manufacturing	5	5	3
Laboratory	5	2	
Shipping	2		

Auditor: _____ Date:_____ Page 1 of 2

Sample 6 (*continued*)

Finding Status Report		
Finding number and date	Finding Summary	Status
List department and audit number and date	Brief description of finding(s). Cite ISO 9000 paragraph(s) or relevant document whenever possible (for example, quality manual, manufacturing third tier).	Cite status
Heat treatment/ 91-11	No procedures for 11/12/91 nonconformances ISO 9001/4.13.	Open
Manufacturing/ 92-11	No work instruction 11/18/92 for corrective action ISO 9001/4.9 and 4.14.	Overdue

Auditor: _____ Date:_____ Page 2 of 2

Conclusions

Internal auditing is an important activity that allows departments to continuously improve their functions. In the very early stages of implementation, trained internal auditors/assessors should provide valuable assistance and advice on how to prepare for registration. Unfortunately, in some cases, internal audits are either not taken seriously or misunderstood. When internal audits are not taken seriously—usually a sign of limited managerial commitment—corrective actions remain pending. Unable or unwilling to correct the system, departments or department heads wrongly assume that it is the responsibility of the internal audit team or the quality manager to address all corrective actions. This is not the case. Internal auditors should not be perceived as police officers or enforcers of the ISO 9000 quality assurance system. Their function is to point out deficiencies, discrepancies, or inaccuracies within the system. Moreover, since they are not directly responsible for the department being audited (as required by paragraph 4.17), they cannot and should not be expected to correct the very nonconformances they raise. These issues are the *direct* responsibility of the noncompliant department.

If the role and function of internal audits are clearly understood by all, much can be gained. Above all, internal audits will help you monitor and achieve readiness. The samples may appear to be cumbersome and difficult to maintain for small companies; however, with the help of a computer and a word processor, all of the forms can easily be computerized and the only effort will be to type your observations. For companies that have a local area network or a wide area network, you may computerize the whole ISO and even use E-mail to schedule your audit and address nonconformances.

When conducted properly, internal quality audits do provide valuable information that should allow you to evaluate the effectiveness of the system. If the system is ineffective, it is the company's responsibility to improve it (see paragraph 4.14 of the ISO 9001–ISO 9003 standards). Internal auditors should always remember that the audit process should be a two-way communication during which information on how to improve the system can be gathered. Internal audits, or first-party audits, should not be confused with third-party audits nor should they necessarily be conducted as third-party audits.

The following chapter offers some suggestions on how to proceed and what to expect in terms of registration cost.

Notes

1. This chapter is an updated version of my chapter 13 from *ISO 9000: Preparing for Registration* (New York: Marcel Dekker and Milwaukee, Wisc.: ASQC Quality Press, 1992) and my chapter 7 from *Implementing the ISO 9000 Series* (New York: Marcel Dekker, 1993). Reprinted from these sources by courtesy of Marcel Dekker, Inc.

2. N. W. Girvin, "Writing Audit Findings: Be Reasonable!" *ASQC Quality Congress Transactions* (Milwaukee, Wisc.: ASQC, 1992), 860.

7 Implementing the Quality Assurance System and Other Considerations

Over the years, I have learned that one of the best ways to begin ISO 9001, ISO 9002, or ISO 9003 implementation is to first focus on the following three paragraphs: 4.1.1, Quality Policy, 4.13, Control of Nonconforming Product, and 4.14, Corrective and Preventive Action. These three paragraphs form an important triad, which, if addressed correctly, will help you build a successful and meaningful quality assurance system (see Figure 7.1). By "addressed correctly," I mean that the three paragraphs, as most other ISO 9000 paragraphs, should be viewed as interrelated, not as independent clauses. Indeed, one of the classic implementation mistakes is to address the standards one paragraph at the time. This is often done by assigning a paragraph or group of paragraphs to one or more individuals or teams. A manager will then periodically monitor the teams' progress. This approach is not effective because it invariably leads to a modular approach of implementation when, in fact, the ISO 9000 series of standards emphasizes a system approach.

One of the major drawbacks of the modular approach is that it leads to a quality assurance model that is likely to be disjointed. An example of what I would call a disjointed or dysfunctional model

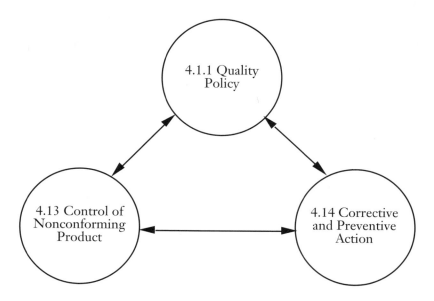

Figure 7.1. The implementation triad.

would be a quality policy that says little, does not reflect reality, or, worse yet, both. Having read countless quality policies that had little to do with the everyday reality of a business, it occurred to me that one of the reasons so many quality assurance systems are inadequate is that they most commonly represent a separate reality than the one expressed in the quality policy or mission statement. In other words, if the quality policy can be viewed as the theory, the quality assurance system represents the approximate reality that barely resembles the theory.

In order to avoid this pitfall and the cynicism of employees that will follow, I urge you to be very careful when you phrase your quality policy. If you do not know where to begin, I suggest that you examine your nonconformities: their type, nature, magnitude, origins, and causes. Simultaneously, begin to think about your preventive and corrective actions: Do you have a method to handle corrective actions? How effective is it? What are your customers complaining about? Why? As you begin to address these issues, always think about your quality policy. If you already have a quality policy, ask yourself if it complements or contradicts your daily performance (nonconformances, corrective and preventive action).

How to Write Quality Policies

One of the difficult tasks faced by many companies is the writing of a quality policy that is relevant to their business. Many people think that a quality policy is a mission statement or vice versa. A mission statement is a statement of objectives that expresses to your employees and your customers your reason for being in business. The quality policy is a subset of the mission statement and should state how the mission statement will be satisfied day in and day out. When a quality policy is confused with a mission statement, it contains a lot of meaningless sentences with an overabundance of unprovable superlatives. The following example will illustrate my point.

> All XYZ products and services will enhance the company's reputation of providing unsurpassed satisfaction through superior quality and premium value.
>
> This will be accomplished by
>
> - Identifying and then exceeding customer expectations with innovative products and services that contribute to the customer's success.
>
> - All XYZ employees sharing a commitment to continuously improve performance and achieve defect-free products and services.
>
> - Developing highly skilled employees with industry-leading abilities.
>
> - Coordinating all applicable disciplines to focus on being the highest quality, lowest cost company in our respective industries.

These statements, which contain many classic TQM phrases such as "exceeding customer expectations," "continuously improve performance," "industry-leading abilities," "highest quality, lowest cost," certainly read very well. But beyond the wonderful prose, how is the validity of these statements proven? What quantitative evidence is there (for example, measurement) that the claims are achieved? How does a company know that the skills of its employees are the highest in the industry? How is quality defined, measured, and proven to be the highest at the lowest cost? Have surveys been conducted? More questions could be asked.

The simplest way to focus on what your quality policy should say is to ask two fundamental questions.

1. What is likely to extremely irritate my customers?

2. What is likely to irritate my customers?

Once you have answered these questions, verify the validity of your answers by asking your customers directly—rather than relying on impersonal surveys—the same questions. You might be surprised by their answers. If their answers do not match your answers, rethink the structure of your quality assurance system.

One way to partly validate your customers' assessment of your overall performance is to analyze their complaints (paragraph 4.14). This will likely lead you to look at your internal nonconformances (4.13), which, in turn, will point to paragraph 4.9, Process Control, and other paragraphs (4.18 and so on). However, you need not apprise everyone of the ISO 9001, ISO 9002, or ISO 9003 paragraph before deciding how your quality policy should be written. Once you know what irritates your customers, you can write a policy that is designed to systematically and continuously reduce the sources (internal and external) of irritation. Finally, as you refine your quality policy, you must try to develop measures (also known as metrics) that will allow you to monitor the effectiveness of the processes required to honor your quality policy/objectives. The quality policies found in chapter 3 generally satisfy these requirements. I encourage you to try to improve upon the policies found in chapter 3; however, as you do, remember that it is relatively easy to write what sounds like a very good quality policy. What is important, however, is not if your policy reads well or pleases an auditor, but whether or not you can honor it on a daily basis, and, more importantly, whether or not it satisfies your customers without driving you out of business! There lies the ultimate challenge.

Having reviewed how to write guidelines and procedures, we turn to implementing a quality assurance system. The implementation process will depend on the state of your quality assurance system. Two strategies are available: top-down or bottom-up (see Figure 7.2). The top-down strategy may be best suited for businesses that have no quality assurance system in place. The strategy tends to force the user to prepare a first draft of the quality manual. This will, in turn, allow the user to determine what supporting documents will be required. The bottom-up strategy may be better suited for organizations that already have a quality assurance system (no matter how incomplete vis-a-vis the ISO 9000 standards). In such cases, it might be more efficient to prepare a list of all the documents, procedures, and records you currently have and see how they might help you satisfy the ISO 9000 requirements. In most cases, you should be able to satisfy 60 percent to 70 percent of the ISO 9000 requirements. Once you have completed this task, determine what is missing and what procedures will need to be written. Now that you can reference all of the appropriate supporting documents, begin writing your quality manual. Using the models provided in chapter 3, you should be able to write your quality manual in a couple of days.

Which Procedures Can Be Included in the Quality Manual?

Most of the procedures relating to the ISO 9001, ISO 9002, or ISO 9003 paragraphs can be included in the quality manual. The sample procedures described in chapters 3 through 5 could be included in a quality manual; however, technical procedures, engineering procedures, and testing procedures should not be included in the quality manual. They are likely to involve very specific steps and may include proprietary information.

There really is no need to follow the structure suggested in Figure 7.2, which identifies four tiers in the quality system. With the exceptions of technical or manufacturing procedures, the quality manual (see chapter 3 and elsewhere in this book) can include most procedures and does not require the development of a special tier of departmental procedures. For most small firms, the quality assurance system could be documented in two to three tiers: the quality manual

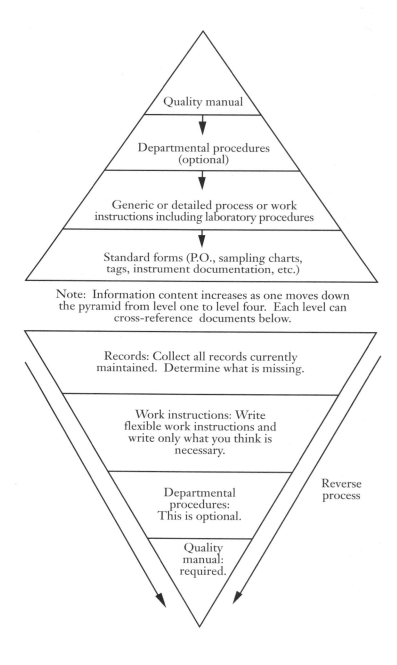

Figure 7.2. Typical implementation strategies.

(tier one), standard operating procedures (tier two), and the supporting forms to record information and data (tier three). In some cases, additional second-tier procedures may have to be written for specific tasks. For example, standard operating procedures written to address some of the requirements of assembly instructions and preventive maintenance (4.9), or testing procedures (4.10.2) should not be included in the quality manual. Such procedures should be included in a separate manual (see Figure 7.3).

As for standard operating procedures, it is difficult to predict how many will be required or to suggest how detailed they should be or even whether or not they are required. It all depends on the nature of your business; the complexity of your processes; whether or not your

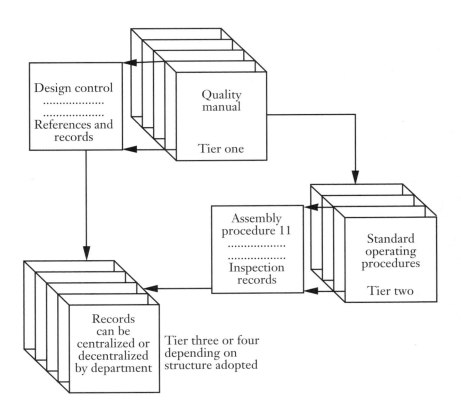

Figure 7.3. Suggested document structure for small businesses.

processes are repetitive; whether or not the standardization of processes is a crucial requirement for the overall quality of your final product; the skills of the operators and assemblers; the training and/ or education required for the job; and a host of other factors. In the case of the dry cleaner, where most processes can be mastered in a couple of hours, the need for standard operating procedures is questionable. On-the-job training is probably adequate. For other jobs— such as welding, electronic testing, chemical analysis, and nursing— varied skills, training, and/or certification may be required. These requirements will vary from country to country and will depend on the level of professionalism or perceived professionalism associated with a particular job. Whenever possible, avoid detailed procedures that limit or restrict someone's ability to operate efficiently.

How Long and How Much for Registration?

This is an often-asked question. Assuming that your organization is seriously committed to achieving ISO 9000 registration and does not constantly shuffle priorities, the implementation process should not, under proper guidance, take longer than six to eight months. This is not likely to happen because companies are easily distracted with the daily chores and activities of running a business and cannot seem to focus on ISO 9000 implementation efforts for more than one or two days at a time. As a result, the number of meetings increases exponentially as people try to recall what was done three weeks ago. As a consultant, I can honestly say that the efficiency and effectiveness of the implementation process can be improved by hiring an experienced consultant whose major tasks would be to evaluate what needs to be done, guide and facilitate the implementation, and ensure that the company remains focused on the various assignments. Hiring a knowledgeable consultant need not cost a fortune. It has been my experience over the past six years that, for small to very small firms, the average number of consulting days ranges between eight to twelve days *depending on the company's motivation and the current status of the quality assurance system.* These estimates, of course, depend on how much you want the consultant to do. If you do not have a quality assurance system in place or only a rudimentary one, it is reasonable to expect that a consultant could spend twice as much time, that is, at least 16–24 days to implement the required quality assurance system. Still, this estimate assumes that the company will also assign some resources to the implementation effort. It is not reasonable to expect a consultant to develop a complete quality assurance system without a significant commitment and participation from management and employees. Also, you should hire a consultant early in the process. There is little a consultant can do after costly mistakes (such as over-documentation) have been made.

The cost of achieving registration will naturally vary depending on the size of your organization. Most registrars base their assessment on two crude estimators: number of employees and square footage of the facilities. These estimators are supposed to indicate how long an audit will take, but do they really? The correlation between square footage or number of employees and the number of activities or processes (the only truly relevant and reliable measure of size to an auditor), is actually very weak. A warehouse that stores a handful of products spread over tens of thousands of square feet could be operated by a crew of 10 to 12 people. A third-party audit, performed by a competent auditor, could easily audit the warehouse in a day. The total number of days, including documentation review and administrative costs, should not exceed two to three days. Yet, if we rely on the primitive algorithm suggested by some questionnaires, the number of audit days could double simply because of the square footage.

Similarly, the number of employees does not always accurately reflect the complexity of a company's processes. Some companies rely on three shifts to make a handful of products that are manufactured by highly automated processes (the chemical industry is one such example). A company could employ 85 employees operating over three shifts—45 employees including administrative and maintenance staff for the morning shift and 20 employees for each of the other two shifts. Moreover, the plant could be spread over 25 acres (or 10 hectares). How many days are required to audit such a plant? Is the number 85 truly representative of the size of the company? Are the 25 acres of any significance? Will the third-party auditors absolutely need to walk throughout every square inch of the 25 acres? Some registrars would argue that six to seven workdays (for example, two auditors and three days) will be required to audit such a facility. Others would argue that four days would be adequate.

European guidelines have been published to estimate the minimum number of days required for an initial assessment. These guidelines are unfair toward small businesses in that they overestimate the audit time required (see Table 7.1).

Most companies with less than 200 or so employees should not require more than five to six days of audit. One of the problems with the minimum estimate published by the European guidelines is that they cite an absolute minimum number of days, for example, three days for 10–14 employees. Three days is not only an overestimation, but it also fails to consider that not all organizations with 10–14 employees perform the same set of functions. It would be much more reasonable to offer a range of audit days rather than an absolute minimum number of days. Also, the arbitrary breakdown of companies into 1–4, 5–9, 10–14, 15–19 employees reflects a misunderstanding about the auditing of small companies. There is, in fact, very little difference between a 5-person organization and a 16-person organization. Both are very small businesses and neither should require more than two days to audit.

I cite these examples to inform the reader that the size of an organization can have a different meaning depending on which registrar you talk to. These interpretations will, in turn, affect the final registration cost. For most small firms with up to 50 or so employees, the three-year registration cost—including two yearly maintenance audits (as opposed to the usual six-month periodic visit arbitrarily suggested by many registrars)—should cost, on average, no more than $8000–$12,000 plus traveling and lodging expenses for the auditors (or approximately $3000–$4000 per year). This assumes the following audit schedule.

- One half day for document review
- Two days of auditing
- One half day for report writing
- One day for first maintenance audit plus a half day for report
- One day for second maintenance audit plus a half day for report

Table 7.1. European guidelines for minimum number of audit days.

Number of employees	Initial assessment	Subsequent annual visit	Reassessment visit	Author's breakdown employees	Author's estimated no. of days
1–4	2	1	1.5	1–14	1.5–2
5–9	2.5	1	1.5	15–29	2–3
10–14	3	1	2	30–59	3–4
15–19	3.5	1	2	60–125	4–5
20–29	4	1.5	3	126–299	5–6
30–59	6	2	4	300–499	6–7
60–99	7	2	4	500–799	7–9
100–249	8	2.5	5	800–1199	9–11*
250–499	10	3	6	1200–1999	11–13*
500–999	12	4	8	2000–3999	13–15*
1000–1999	15	5	10	4000–5999	15–17*
2000–3999	18	6	12	6999–9999	17–20*
4000–7999	21	7	14		
8.000+	24	8	16		

* For companies over 800 or 1000, the issue of multiple sites needs to be considered.
Source: Quality System Update 5, no. 5 (1995): 12.

A total of six days at an average of $1000 per day is $6000. Administrative fees (if applied) for the three-year period would be $3000 to $6000.

Selecting a registrar need not be as complicated as some consultants would have you believe. You don't need intricate matrices to help you decide which registrar to select. If you export many of your products to Europe, you may (but not necessarily) want to use a European registrar; however, if you have little or no exposure to the European market, European registrars are of little significance nor should they be perceived as being better than national registrars. People often ask me, "But what if the registrar goes out of business two or three years from now, what happens then?" Nothing extraordinary; you simply shop around for another registrar. I am sure you will very quickly find one that matches your needs.

Having described how a quality assurance system can easily be implemented to satisfy the ISO 9000 series, Part II focuses on what techniques and tools are available to assist you with the implementation and maintenance of your quality assurance system.

Note

1. Some registrars could probably lower the fees by as much as 15 percent.

Part II

Helpful Techniques

Introduction

The techniques presented in the following chapters are presented only as tools that *could* be used to address specific requirements of the ISO 9000 standards. Many of these techniques, such as SPC and design of experiments, were developed in the 1920s and 1930s. Most of the other techniques are at least 20 years old. Still, old does not necessarily mean out-of-date. In fact, many of these techniques have proven themselves over the years and can be considered reliable.

As has been repeatedly stated, the ISO 9000 standards—unlike automotive standards such as QS-9000—do not (yet) require you to use any particular technique. Many, but not all, of the tools or techniques presented in chapters 8–18 are mentioned in the ISO 9004 guidelines; however, no explanation is given as to how these techniques may or may not be applied. The few techniques presented in the following chapters represent a sample of the multitude of techniques available. Most of these techniques can be used in series, that is, one technique leading to another, which leads to yet another. For example, the use of a Pareto diagram may lead a team to investigate a problem using a cause-and-effect diagram. This may in turn suggest a gauge R&R study.

The techniques are included for reference and can help you maintain an effective quality assurance system. I encourage you to test the usefulness of these tools. As is the case with any new idea or process, it is your responsibility to validate the effectiveness and suitability of the tool. Most techniques look attractive on paper, but, when applied, are found to be ponderous or cumbersome and of limited value (quality function deployment would probably fit the classification of a ponderous technique). On the other hand, you may discover that the tool, simple as it may be, is very valuable and will help you quantify information and reach better informed decisions

(Pareto charts and cause-and-effect diagrams, for example). Finally, note that the techniques presented in Part II can be used by any organization, small or large. Most of them can be implemented by an individual; others are more effective with teams. If a team is required, a two- or three-person team is often adequate. If you wish to learn more about any of these techniques and many more, I suggest that you consult the following books.

J. M. Juran and F. M. Gryna Jr., *Juran's Quality Control Handbook* 4 ed. (New York: McGraw-Hill, 1974). This handbook covers just about every quality topic imaginable. It is still the best reference available and has been translated into many languages.

D. C. Montgomery, *Introduction to Statistical Quality Control* (New York: John Wiley & Sons, 1985). This is an excellent source with many examples; however, the author assumes a good knowledge of mathematics on the part of the reader.

N. R. Tague, *The Quality Toolbox* (Milwaukee, Wisc.: ASQC Quality Press, 1995). This book includes a tool matrix to help you find the right tool to solve a particular problem or achieve a certain goal.

8　Acceptance Sampling

Potential ISO 9000 Application: Paragraph 4.10.2

Some form of receiving inspection for raw materials, semifinished goods, assembled components, or finished goods is required by paragraph 4.10.2 of ISO 9001, ISO 9002, and ISO 9003. It has been my experience that the preferred method used by probably 50 percent of all U.S. companies is still acceptance sampling (as defined by MIL-STD-105D, recently updated to the letter E), the well-known statistical technique developed for the U.S. military in the 1930s. From an auditing point of view, the problem with MIL-STD-105D is not so much the technique, but, rather, its dubious and sometimes incorrect application. The purpose of this section is to present the reader with a brief overview of the technique.[1]

Acceptance sampling should only be used if the purpose of the inspection is to either accept, reject, or, perhaps, dispose of a product or lot. This process is often referred to as *lot sentencing*. Lots are either accepted for production or subject to some form of lot disposition, which may include having the lot returned to the vendor, supplier, or subcontractor. Acceptance sampling does not estimate the quality of the lot nor does the technique provide for any direct form of quality control. Since the lot sentencing decision is based on sampling a lot, the decision can never be absolute and is, therefore, based on probabilities. Consequently, whenever a lot is sentenced (subject to acceptance or rejection), the customer accepting the lot and the vendor or subcontractor submitting the lot are exposed to two inter-related risks known as the *producer's risk* and the *consumer's risk*.

Producer's risk: The producer's risk, denoted by the Greek letter alpha (α), is the probability that a good lot will be rejected by the customer's receiving inspection sampling plan.

Consumer's risk: The consumer's risk, denoted by the Greek letter beta (β), is the probability that a bad lot will be accepted by the customer's acceptance sampling plan.

Expanding on these definitions, one realizes that one of the major disadvantages of acceptance sampling is that a supplier could submit two lots of identical quality levels, that is, two lots with the same percentage of defective parts, and the customer may accept one lot and reject the other! Acceptance should therefore be viewed as an audit tool to ensure that the output of a process conforms to requirements.

Simplified Procedure for Using MIL-STD-105D

MIL-STD-105D is a widely used acceptance sampling system for attributes (that is, good or bad product). The standard provides for three types of sampling: single sampling, double sampling, and multiple sampling. Moreover, for each type of sampling plan, one can select either normal inspection, tightened inspection, or reduced inspection. The following simplified description only covers single normal inspection.

1. Choose the average quality level (AQL). The AQL represents the poorest level of quality—denoted in percentage (0.01, 0.05, 0.5, 1.0, or higher)—for the vendor's process that the customer would consider to be acceptable as a process average. The concept of AQL is difficult to comprehend or accept in today's expectation of 100 percent quality. The AQL indicates that the customer is willing to accept from a supplier, for example, an average of one percent or more defective parts or assemblies. Corrective actions are only required from the supplier, vendor, or subcontractor whenever a lot is found to be unacceptable. Still, as will be demonstrated, an AQL can be set as low as 0.010 per-

cent. For such low percentages, the supplier's or subcontractor's processes must be very capable in the statistical sense of the word (see chapter 17 on SPC).

Selecting an appropriate AQL level is not always easy. You cannot simply select an arbitrarily low AQL level without some prior knowledge of the capability of your supplier(s). Similarly, there is no need to select an arbitrarily high level (above 10 percent) just to please or help a supplier. Finally, you cannot apply the same high or low AQL level (as is often done) to all of your suppliers or subcontractors. This assumes that all of your suppliers or subcontractors perform at the same level of quality, which is very unlikely. In order to select an appropriate AQL level for each supplier, you first need to obtain some data that will allow you to measure performance. The selection of the appropriate measure is up to you (on-time delivery, number of violations per month, number of rejected parts per lot, number of incomplete deliveries, and so on). Once you have accumulated and analyzed some data, you can then attempt to set a preliminary AQL level and adjust it up or down depending on performance. Ironically, one of the methods you or your suppliers could use to monitor process performance is SPC (see chapter 17 for application and limitations).

2. Determine the lot size.

3. Select the type of sampling (single, double, or multiple). Only single sampling is reproduced here.

4. Select the inspection level (I = reduced, II = normal, III = tightened).

5. Knowing the lot size and the inspection level, obtain a letter code from Table 8.1.

6. From the code letter, AQL, and type of sampling, read the sampling plan from Table 8.2, which tells you the maximum number of items that can be found defective before the lot must be rejected.

Example. Suppose that a vendor supplies parts in lots of 20 parts. Suppose further that the contract (see ISO 9001, ISO 9002, or ISO 9003 paragraph 4.3) calls for an AQL of 0.010 percent (near perfection). What would be your acceptance plan? From Table 8.1, we see that a normal inspection plan (II) for a lot size of 16–25 calls for a

Table 8.1. Sample size code letters.

Lot or batch size	General inspection levels		
	I	II	III
2 to 8	A	A	B
9 to 15	A	B	C
16 to 25	B	C	E
26 to 50	C	D	E
51 to 90	C	E	F
91 to 150	D	F	G
151 to 280	E	G	H
281 to 500	F	H	J
501 to 1,200	G	J	K
1,201 to 3,200	H	K	L
3,201 to 10,000	J	L	M
10,001 to 35,000	K	M	N
35,000 to 150,000	L	N	P
150,001 to 500,000	M	P	Q
500,001 and over	N	Q	R

sampling letter of C. Table 8.2 indicates that a code letter of C calls for a sample size of five items. Upon reception of the batch from your supplier you would select five parts at random and perform the required inspection test as specified in your inspection plan, procedures, or contract (see 4.3 and/or 4.10.2 of ISO 9001, ISO 9002, or ISO 9003). If all parts pass the acceptance—in other words, zero reject—accept the lot. If one or more part(s) is/are found to be unacceptable, the lot *should* be rejected.

I emphasize *should* because it has been my experience that even if a batch must be rejected, it is not. The reasons given for not rejecting a lot that should be rejected are very creative and occasionally illogical. People will often resample a lot in the hope that the lot will be accepted the second time. If you do not really want to reject/return a

Table 8.2. Reduced MIL-STD-105D master table for normal inspection (single sampling).*

Sample size code letter	Sample size	Acceptable quality level (AQL) Numbers less than 10 are interpreted as percent defective. Numbers greater than 10 are interpreted as defects per hundred units.						
		0.010	0.10	1.0	2.5	25	100	250
		Ac Re	Ac Re	Ac Re	Ac Re	Ac Re	Ac Re	Ac Re
A	2	⇓	⇓	⇓	⇓	1 2	5 6	10 11
B	3	⇓	⇓	⇓	⇓	2 3	7 8	14 15
C	5	⇓	⇓	⇓	0 1	3 4	10 11	21 22
D	8	⇓	⇓	⇓	0 1	5 6	14 15	30 31
E	13	⇓	⇓	0 1	1 2	7 8	21 22	44 45
F	20	⇓	⇓	0 1	1 2	10 11	21 22	44 45
G	32	⇓	⇓	1 2	2 3	14 15	⇑	⇑
H	50	⇓	⇓	1 2	3 4	21 22	⇑	⇑
J	80	⇓	⇓	2 3	5 6	21 22	⇑	⇑
K	125	⇓	0 1	3 4	7 8	21 22	⇑	⇑
L	200	⇓	0 1	5 6	10 11	21 22	⇑	⇑
M	315	⇓	1 2	7 8	14 15	21 22	⇑	⇑
N	500	⇓	1 2	10 11	21 22	21 22	⇑	⇑
P	800	⇓	2 3	14 15	21 22	21 22	⇑	⇑
Q	1250	0 1	3 4	21 22	21 22	21 22	⇑	⇑
R	2000	0 1	5 6	21 22	21 22	21 22	⇑	⇑

* The full table contains 26 AQL levels. I have only reproduced eight of the 26 AQLs.

Legend:

⇓ = Use the first sampling plan below arrow. If sample size equals or exceeds lot or batch size, do 100 percent inspection.

⇑ = Use first sampling plan above arrow.

Ac = Acceptance number

Re = Rejection number

lot, then why waste time inspecting parts? Resampling for the purpose of accepting a lot is an incorrect application of acceptance sampling. Third-party auditors throughout the world routinely witness this unfortunate practice. When they do observe such misapplications of internal (or other) procedures, they have no alternative but to note the occurrence, and, if the occurrence is repeatedly observed, issue a nonconformance. This could eventually jeopardize issuance of a certificate.

Rather than continue with the incorrect application of a procedure, the appropriate solution would be to review the acceptance sampling process and decide whether or not it should be modified and under what conditions (see corrective action paragraph 4.14).

Example. A vendor periodically provides you with lots of 1000 parts. The AQL was contractually agreed to be no more than 25 defects per lot, where a defect is defined as *any* mutually agreed upon, but well-defined, imperfections (as specified in the contract) such as scratches, incorrect invoice order, incorrect count, or other criteria. Proceeding with Tables 8.1 and 8.2 we find that

> Letter code = J
>
> Sample size = 80
>
> For an AQL of 25, we read Table 8.2 to determine that we would need to find 22 defects before rejecting the lot of 1000 parts.

This acceptance sampling procedure could be used as second- or third-tier procedure to satisfy the intent of paragraph 4.10 (especially, 4.10.2 and 4.20.2). I say "could be used," because not every company needs to use MIL-STD-105D. A dry cleaning store will not likely need to implement MIL-STD-105D. The volume of receiving inspection (a few gallons of chemicals per month) does not warrant the use and cost associated with such applications. If you should decide to use some form of acceptance sampling, however, the employee in charge of using the application must be able to apply the technique correctly and consistently, as required per paragraph 4.20.2, which states: "The supplier shall establish and maintain documented procedures to implement and control the application of the statistical techniques identified in 4.20.1."

Notes

1. For further information on acceptance sampling, see E. G. Schilling and D. J. Sommers, "Acceptance Sampling," in J. M. Juran and F. M. Gryna, *Juran's Quality Control Handbook* (New York: McGraw-Hill, 1974), and D. C. Montgomery, *Introduction to Statistical Quality Control* (New York: John Wiley & Sons, 1985).

2. Each registrar has its own set of rules regarding the issuance of nonconformances and the number of noncomformances that can be issued before issuance of a certificate is withheld.

9   Problem Definition

Potential ISO 9000 Application: Paragraphs 4.4, 4.6, 4.9, 4.10, 4.13, 4.14, 4.15, and 4.17

One of the most difficult issues surrounding the continuous improvement process is the problem statement. Formulating a good problem statement is the key to solving most problems. Whereas a bad problem statement can undermine any subsequent attempts to solve a problem, a well-defined problem is often half solved. Consequently, whenever an individual or a team is confronted with a problem, it should try to focus and define the problem by asking the following questions.

What is the problem?

When does it occur?

Where does it occur?

Who is affected?

How are people or functions affected?

How much does it cost?

The essential element of a good problem statement is a concise declaration that attempts to answer these questions. A good problem statement describes in specific, concrete terms what is wrong. It describes the present undesirable situation while avoiding hidden solutions. A good problem statement should

- State the effect(s). It states what is wrong, not why it is wrong.

- Focus on the gap between what is and what should be. The gap may be a change, or deviation, from the norm, standard, or reasonable expectation.

- Have measures that could identify how often the problem occurs, when it occurs (time of day or of month, for example), and how much it is estimated to cost (internal and external cost, if possible). This last step is important when determining how many resources should be allocated to solve the problem.

- Be specific and avoid broad categories of causes such as "employee morale or motivation," "poor productivity," "inadequate communication," or "poor training." These statements have a different meaning to different people.

- Avoid statements with the words "a lack of." Such statements imply that a solution already exists (although in some cases a solution may indeed exist but no one listened). Also, try to avoid stating a problem as a question. This may imply that the answer to the question is the solution.

- Focus on how people or areas are affected by the problem.

Examples of Bad Problem Statements
What is wrong with the following problem statements?

- Excessive handling
- Too high a scrap rate
- Too many operator delays (or operator delays)
- Excessive engineering drawing revisions
- Too much time spent processing delays
- Poor motivation among the operators
- Not enough machine utilization
- How to say *no* to nonprojected work

The last statement suggests a solution. The basic problem is the inability to complete projected work. The statement could be rephrased as follows: "Trying to meet unexpected demands interferes with completion of projected work during second quarter of the year."

Another example of a poor problem statement is: "Lack of central filing system causes duplication in training cost." This statement assumes that a central system is the solution to the problem. The real problem is a duplication in training cost. The statement could be rephrased as follows: "Duplication exists in costs for training programs, materials, and personnel."

Examples of More Focused Problem Statements
These problem statements get to the heart of the problem.

- The computer system was down 32 hours more than average in August.

- Data entry overtime cost is 20 percent over budget.

- Customer complaints are up 13 percent since last quarter.

For all of these problem statements, one can begin to ask: "What could *cause* this problem to occur?" For some problems, the eventual root cause(s) can eventually be discovered by repeatedly asking why whenever a legitimate cause has been identified (this is known as the rule of five whys).

Supporting techniques: cause-and-effect diagrams, Pareto diagrams, failure mode and effects analysis.

10   Flowcharts

Potential ISO 9000 Application: Paragraph 4.9a or Whenever a Process or Method Needs to Be Described

Flowcharts can sometimes be better than written instructions. A flowchart is an excellent way to reveal flaws in a process that could not be easily detected in a written procedure. The typical flowchart symbols listed in Figure 10.1 are suggestions. To my knowledge, there are no international standards for flowchart symbols. I have included a couple of examples to demonstrate how processes can be described using a flowchart. As with any other technique, flowcharting is not appropriate for every situation. One of the advantages of flowcharting is that it can often be an excellent opportunity to critically review a process. As one flowcharts a process, the opportunity to improve or modify a traditional method or a routine work flow should always be looked for. A tortuous flow diagram with many paths crossing each other or numerous inspections or decision points may be an indication that a process is not efficient and could be optimized further. Try to apply the technique to a couple of applications before reaching a final decision (see Figures 10.2 and 10.3).

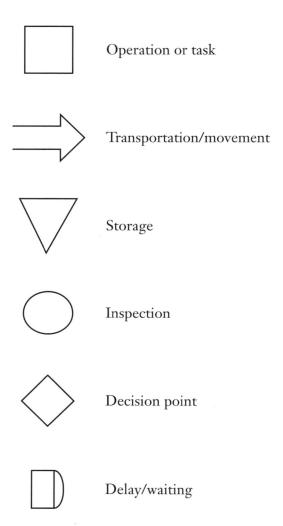

Figure 10.1. Typical flowchart symbols.

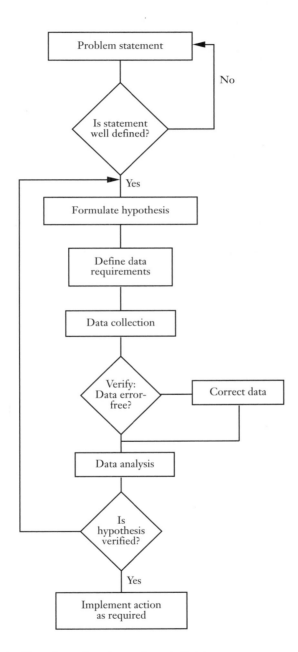

Figure 10.2. Flowchart showing a data definition process.

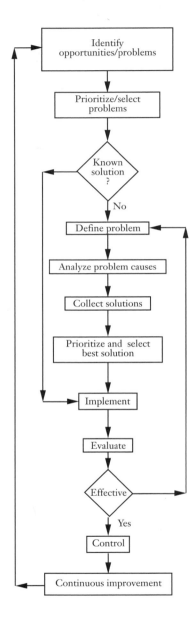

Figure 10.3. Flowchart showing a problem-solving process.

11　Gauge Repeatability and Reproducibility Study

Potential ISO 9000 Application:
Paragraph 4.11.2a

Measurements are never exact. They are subject to at least two sources of variation and thus errors: instrument inaccuracy and operator experience/skill. Instrument inaccuracy may be caused by mishandling or dropping the instrument, or an out-of-calibration condition. Operator inexperience or inadequate skill level may also lead to some misreading and thus measurement errors. In cases where the measurement needs to be in the $\frac{1}{1000}$ or $\frac{1}{10,000}$, such errors may be costly for they may lead to unexpected or unnecessary costs in repair and rework. Gauge R&R studies are designed to help you determine if your instruments are statistically capable of detecting or discriminating the required changes/variations as defined by engineering or other functions. Before proceeding any further, let us first define some key concepts.[1]

- *Gauge accuracy* is the difference between the observed average of measurements and the master value. The master value can be determined by averaging several measurements with the most accurate measuring equipment available.

- *Gauge repeatability* is the variation in measurements obtained with one gauge when used several times by one operator while measuring identical characteristics on the same parts.

- *Gauge reproducibility* is the variation in the average of the measurements made by different operators using the same gauge when measuring identical characteristics on the same parts.

- *Gauge stability* (or drift) is the total variation in measurements obtained with a gauge on the same master or master parts when measuring a single characteristic over an extended time period.

- *Gauge linearity* is the difference in the accuracy values through the expected operating range of the gauge.

Computing Gauge Repeatability and Reproducibility

The following two tables are based on data and calculations found in *Measurement System Analysis: Reference Manual* distributed by the Automotive Industry Action Group. The method described here, or a similar one, is required for all suppliers to Ford, Chrysler, and General Motors who will be required to achieve QS-9000 registration. Gauge R&R studies are time-consuming and, therefore, expensive to perform. Although statistical software is available to perform the computation described, one must allocate the time and money to collect the data. Gauge R&R studies are certainly valuable studies, but each organization must decide how much time and effort it is willing to allocate to the project. One should also consider whether a gauge R&R study is necessary. A dry cleaning store will not likely need to know how accurate and precise its thermometers are. A manufacturer of precision equipment, however, would probably consider conducting gauge R&R studies. Similarly, if your company is contractually required to satisfy small tolerances for certain key process parameters, you must be able to demonstrate that your measurement system is capable of measuring these tolerances. In cases where the manufacturer of precision equipment actually produces equipment that is used as a standard by others, it might be very difficult to actually verify the accuracy of the standard since no reference instrument of higher precision is available.

As always, the techniques presented herewith are nothing more than tools that could be used to satisfy one or more of the requirements stated in the ISO 9000 standards. Many other tools are available; choose the one that best suits your needs.

Table 11.1. Gauge R&R examples and computations.

Trial/operator	Parts										Average $\bar{X}$
	1	2	3	4	5	6	7	8	9	10	
A 1	0.65	1.00	0.85	0.85	0.55	1.00	0.95	0.85	1.00	0.60	0.83
2	0.60	1.00	0.80	0.90	0.45	1.00	0.95	0.80	1.00	0.70	0.83
3											
Average	0.63	1.00	0.83	0.90	0.50	1.00	0.95	0.83	1.00	0.65	$\bar{X}_a = 0.83$
Range	0.05	0.00	0.05	0.10	0.10	0.00	0.00	0.05	0.05	0.10	$R_a = 0.05$
B 1	0.55	1.05	0.80	0.80	0.40	1.00	0.95	0.75	1.00	0.55	0.79
2	0.55	0.95	0.75	0.75	0.40	1.05	0.90	0.70	0.95	0.50	0.75
3											
Average	0.55	1.00	0.78	0.78	0.40	1.03	0.93	0.73	0.98	0.53	$\bar{X}_b = 0.77$
Range	0.00	0.10	0.05	0.05	0.00	0.05	0.05	0.05	0.05	0.05	$R_b = 0.05$
C 1	0.50	1.05	0.80	0.80	0.45	1.00	0.95	0.80	1.05	0.85	0.83
2	0.55	1.00	0.80	0.80	0.50	1.05	0.95	0.80	1.05	0.80	0.83
3											
Average	0.53	1.03	0.80	0.80	0.48	1.03	0.95	0.80	1.05	0.83	$\bar{X}_c = 0.83$
Range	0.05	0.05	0.00	0.00	0.05	0.05	0.00	0.00	0.00	0.05	$R_c = 0.03$
Part Avg. $\bar{X}_p$	0.57	1.01	0.80	0.83	0.46	1.02	0.94	0.78	1.01	0.67	$R_p = 0.56$

$[R_a = 0.05 + R_b = 0.05 + R_c = 0.03]/[\text{Number of operators} = 3] = \bar{R} = 0.04$ $\bar{R} = 0.04$

$[\text{Max } \bar{X} = 0.83 - \text{Min } \bar{X} = 0.77] = \bar{X} \text{ difference} = 0.06$ 0.06

$[\bar{R} = 0.04 \times D_4 = 3.27] = UCL_R = 0.13$ 0.13

$[\bar{R} = 0.04 \times D_3 = 0.00] = LCL_R = 0.00$ 0.00

$D_4 = 3.27$ for two trials or two operators and 2.58 for three trials or three operators

Example. The trial/operator column shown in Table 11.1 indicates the number of trials or operators used to perform the gauge study. The example below shows three operators (A, B, and C) measuring 10 parts twice (the replication is thus equal to 2). Unlike other statistical techniques, the following method does not compute gauge R&R based on tolerance. Rather, the technique relies on part variation (PV) for its estimation. [Note: Averages for operator B and C are not entered in the table and should be computed by the reader.]

It is important that each operator measures all parts at the same location. Before conducting an R&R study, you must mark all parts to indicate where the measurements will be made. The technique assumes that all operators know how to use the instrument and have similar skill levels. If you should have statistically significant operator variation, the technique will help you detect which operator is out-of-control. See also ANOVA techniques in chapter 18.

The study in Table 11.2 indicates that the variation in gauge R&R consumes approximately 25 percent of the total variation in parts. The gauge is therefore deemed acceptable. What would an R&R of 80% indicate? (Note: Some R&R studies have shown that the %R&R exceeds 100 percent!)

SPC can also be used to assess gauge capability. For further information see Donald J. Wheeler and Richard W. Lyday, *Evaluating the Measurement Process*, second edition.

Note

1. *Measurement Systems Analysis: Reference Manual* (Southfield, Mich: Automotive Industry Action Group, 1991).

Table 11.2. Sample computation for gauge R&R.

Part number and name: <u>Gasket</u>_____ Date: <u>February 10, 1995</u>
Gauge name: <u>Micrometer</u>_____ Gauge number: <u>10-1022-33</u>
Specifications: 0.6–1.0 mm   Gauge type: 0.0–10.1 mm
Characteristic: Thickness
Study perfomed by:_____
From previous data sheet (see Table 11.1): $\bar{R}$ = 0.04, X difference = 0.06, Rp = 0.56

Measurement Unit Analysis	% Process Variation

Repeatabilty—equipment variation (EV)
 	
$EV \doteq \bar{R} \times K_1$ Trials K_1
 	
  $= 0.04 \times 4.56$ 2   4.56
 	
  $= 0.18$ 3   3.05
	%EV = 100[EV/TV]
	  = 100[0.18/0.93]
	  = 18.7%

Reproducibility—appraiser variation (AV)
 	
$AV = \sqrt{[X\mathrm{diff} \times K_2]^2 - \left[\dfrac{EV^2}{nr}\right]}$
 	
  Where n = number of parts
  R = number of replications
 	
$AV = \sqrt{[0.06 \times 2.70]^2 - \left[\dfrac{0.18^2}{10 \times 2}\right]} = 0.16$
 	
  Operators   2   3
    K_2 3.65   2.70
	%AV = 100(AV/TV)
	  = 100(0.16/0.93)
	  = 16.8%

Repeatability and reproducibility (R&R)
 	
$R\&R = \sqrt{[EV^2 + AV^2]}$
 	
  $= \sqrt{[0.18^2 + 0.16^2]}$
 	
  $= 0.24$
	%R&R = 100(R&R/TV)
	  = 100(0.24/0.93)
	  = 25.2% (acceptable)
	Guidelines:
	1) Less than 10% gauge is fine.
	2) 0–30% gauge should be acceptable for most applications.
	3) Over 30% gauge system needs improvement.

Table 11.2. *(continued)*

Measurement Unit Analysis			% Process Variation
Part variation (PV)	Parts	K_3	%PV = 100(PV/TV)
PV = Rp × K_3	2	3.65	= 100(0.90/0.93)
= 0.56 × 1.62	3	2.70	= 96.8%
= 0.90	4	2.30	
	5	2.08	
	6	1.93	
	7	1.82	
	8	1.74	
	9	1.67	
	10	1.62	
Total variation (TV)			
$TV = \sqrt{[R\&R^2 + PV^2]}$			
$= \sqrt{[0.24^2 + 0.90^2]}$			
$= 0.93$			

12   Failure Mode and Effects Analysis

Potential ISO 9000 Application: Paragraphs 4.4 and 4.14

As its name implies, failure mode and effects analysis (FMEA) is a technique that allows an individual or problem-solving team to analyze potential or actual failure modes of an event. The event can be a process (process FMEA), a product (product FMEA), a project, or a procedure. The technique has been popular for quite a few years among automotive suppliers and is a required analytical tool specified by the joint Quality System Requirements (QS-9000) of Chrysler, Ford, and General Motors. Variations of the technique have been used by the food industry and may be used for environmental impact studies.

The analysis begins by subjectively evaluating each potential cause of the failure on a scale of 1–5. The evaluation is measured using three criteria: frequency of occurrence, severity of the occurrence to individual(s) or property damage (which could be measured in dollars lost) or combination of both, and probability of detection prior to delivery or failure of the product, completion of the project, or event in general. Having estimated each criterion, a risk priority number (RPN) is then computed by multiplying the estimated frequency, severity, and detection (see following examples). It is suggested that the failure mode with the highest RPN is first addressed (however, see upcoming warning). Next, solutions are proposed (see cause-and-effect diagram), tested, and verified, and a new RPN number is computed to see if actions taken result in a lower RPN.

FMEA can be used to analyze

- **Procedures**

    Manufacturing/assembly

    Receiving inspection, for example, to analyze why defective products are accepted

    Testing procedures which fail to detect errors

    Health and safety procedures

- **Processes**

    Maintenance

    Assembly

    Inspection

    Administrative

    Sales/marketing

- **Projects**

    Design engineering

    Manufacturing engineering

    Testing engineering

    Software engineering

    Hardware engineering

- **Products**

    To analyze potential or actual failures and impact on users

It should be noted that for complex projects, processes, or products, FMEA quickly becomes a huge undertaking. One difficulty with FMEAs is that the various evaluations for frequency, severity, and detection are often guesses or estimations based on little or no objective evidence or data. In such cases, the quality of the estimates can be improved with a team of experienced individuals. Each team member is allowed to vote and a consensus is reached. FMEA does not require large teams in order to be effective.

The following percentages can be used as estimates or guidelines to quantify the frequency of occurrence. Figures are based on the negative exponential frequency distribution, which assumes that causes/events are distributed following a Poisson distribution.

Occurrence	Probability
Very low (1)	< 0.5%
Somewhat low (2)	0.5–5%
Average (3)	5.1–15%
Somewhat high (4)	15.1–40%
High (5)	>40.0%

Common sense should be used when applying FMEA. For example, these guidelines state that the failure mode with the highest RPN number should be selected first for investigation. But is that necessarily true in all cases? Suppose, for example, that after performing an FMEA a team arrives at the following RPN numbers.

$$S \times F \times D = \text{RPN}$$
$$2 \times 3 \times 4 = 24 \ (1)$$
$$1 \times 2 \times 5 = 10 \ (2)$$
$$5 \times 1 \times 2 = 10 \ (3)$$

Our guidelines tell us that we should investigate the first failure (RPN of 24) mode, but what about the third mode, which has an RPN of only 10 but a safety hazard of 5? Obviously, the simple formula does not always offer good guidance. The formula could perhaps be improved by weighing each factor (S, F, and D) with a coefficient whose value should be determined by each team. See Figure 12.1 for a sample FMEA.

Prepared by: _____   Date: _____
Function: _____
FMEA identification number: _____

Mode of failure or potential failure mode	Effects of failure	Degree of severity S	Cause of potential cause of failure	Frequency of occurrence F	Chance of detection D	Risk priority number RPN = $F \times S \times D$	Actions taken	New RPN
Car will not start. Instrument will not read. Errors are not detected.	Owner will be irritated. Analysis is not performed. Operator must fix problem.	Severity: 1 = Insignificant loss to user, 5 = Major safety hazard	• Electrical failure • Instrument dropped • Operator not trained	Frequency of occurrence: 1 = Rare occurrence, 5 = Almost certain to occur	Detection 1 = Certain 5 = Unlikely	Examples: $S = 1$ $F = 2$ $D = 5$ RPN = $1 \times 2 \times 5 = 10$	This can involve redesigning a part to reduce a risk or redesigning a process to eliminate or reduce a problem.	Is action effective? If so, the RPN should be reduced, thus validating the action.

Mode of failure or potential failure mode	Effects of failure	Degree of severity S	Cause of potential cause of failure	Frequency of occurrence F	Chance of detection D	Risk priority number RPN = $F \times S \times D$	Actions taken	New RPN
			The technique of cause-and-effect analysis could be used here.			24 10 5		

Figure 12.1. Example of a failure mode and effects analysis.

13   Cause-and-Effect Diagrams (Ishikawa Diagrams)

Potential ISO 9000 Application:
Paragraphs 4.13 and 4.14

Cause-and-effect diagrams are a simple, but effective technique that can be used once a problem has been clearly identified (see chapter 9) and causes must then be postulated. The technique is best used with a team of two to six individuals. Larger teams are more difficult to manage. A common assumption often made when using cause-and-effect diagrams is that problems (or opportunities to improve, as some would say) are often attributable to four major causes: man (operator), machine, method, or material; each, a potential source of process variability (see Figure 13.1). Naturally, one is not limited to these major causes. Figure 13.2 illustrates how the technique works.

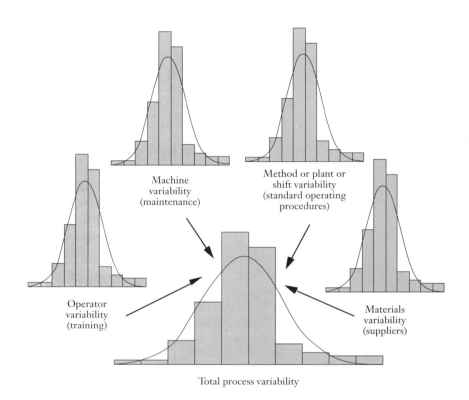

Total process variability

Figure 13.1. Potential sources of process variablility.

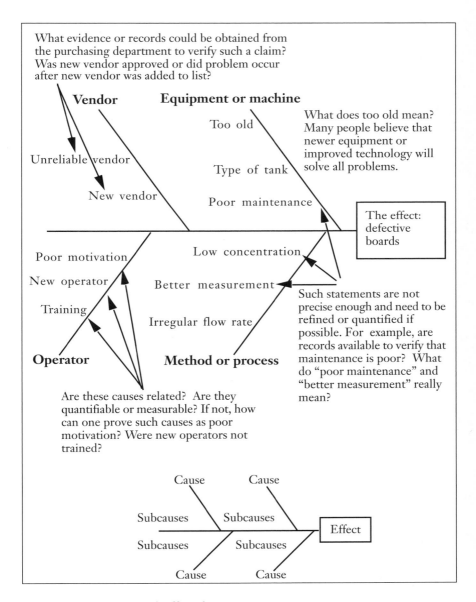

Figure 13.2. Cause-and-effect diagram.

14   Data Collection

The importance of data collection is recognized by the ISO 9000 standards. Paragraph 15.1 of ISO 9004-1 guidelines states that: "The implementation of corrective action begins with the detection of a quality-related problem and involves taking measures to eliminate or minimize the recurrence of the problem."[1]

One of the main objectives for the collection of data is to help people achieve better decisions and verify the validity of the proposed solutions. The collection of data also allows individuals to rely on the scientific process to investigate problems within the context of hypothesis testing. (A formal development of the statistical subject of hypothesis testing is beyond the scope of this introductory book.) Hypotheses consist of propositions stated in terms that can be verified in quantifiable terms. The following statements are hypotheses.

The average weight of men is 170 lbs. (77 kgs).

The number of defective parts averages 50 per month.

A pressure vessel can withstand pressures of up to 100 psi.

Our processes are statistically capable ($C_{pk} = 1.35$).

One of the advantages of formulated hypotheses is that they can be verified/tested using a broad range of statistical techniques. Before verifying hypotheses, however, one must first collect data. *Data* are a source of information needed to optimize a decision process.

What Is Involved in Data Collection

Why collect data? We collect data to obtain quantitative information to answer specific questions.

How do I collect data? Gather your data very carefully! First prepare a data collection sheet where you will identify each variable to be measured. Poorly collected data invariably lead to costly mistakes. Data collection is often an expensive proposition. Like any other process, it must be planned, verified (for accuracy), and thoughtfully analyzed. Too much data are collected either for no apparent purpose, for the wrong reasons, or simply to satisfy an ill-defined question (hypothesis) or problem statement.

How much data should be collected? Only gather as much data as needed and for as long as it is needed. Proper sampling can help reduce the cost of data collection without compromising statistical accuracy, parameter estimation, and validation of hypotheses. Of course, the larger the sample the better the accuracy of the estimation, but also the greater the collection and analysis cost.

From where do I collect data? Whenever data must be collected, consider the possible sources of variation in the data. Examples of sources of variation include different operators, shifts, location, environmental conditions, method, type of processes, type of equipment, suppliers, time of day, day of the week, type of catalyst, and instrument error. See paragraph 4.11.2 of ISO 9001 and chapter 13 of this book.

Types of data. Data can be either quantitative or qualitative. Quantitative data can be measured with an instrument or counted. Measured data could be measured using a scale, a pH meter, a viscosity meter, a thermometer, a voltmeter, an oscilloscope, a flow meter, a flux meter, a pressure gauge, a questionnaire or survey, or so on. Counted quantitative data include such characteristics as number of scratches per part, number of defects per lot or batches, number of rejects per shift, and so forth. Qualitative data can be categorized by color (red or green), type of operator (male or female), type of machine (lathe 566 vs. lathe 756), shift (first, second, or third), subjective categorization (good, bad), and so on.

Regardless of the type data collected, in order to be of any value to the analyst, the data must be correct and relevant to the problem or hypothesis. Whenever possible,

1. Always strive to learn something from the data.

2. Try to witness the data collection or, better yet, collect the data yourself.

Note

1. ISO 9004-1:1994, paragraph 15.1.

15   Pareto Diagrams

Potential ISO 9000 Application: Paragraphs 4.9, 4.10, 4.13, 4.14, and 4.17

The Pareto principle (named after the nineteenth-century Italian economist Vilfredo Pareto), formulated by J. M. Juran several decades ago, states that "a *few* contributors to the cost are responsible for *the bulk* of the cost. These vital few contributors need to be identified so that quality improvement resources can be concentrated in those areas."[1] A Pareto analysis is very useful to identify potential problem areas. See Figure 15.1 for an example of Pareto analysis.

A company produces printed circuit boards that are processed through four tanks. Recently, the percentage of defective boards jumped from a yearly average of less than 3.8 percent to 9.0 percent. A simple study was conducted to categorize defective boards by tanks. Boards were classified as defective if they failed a functional test after being processed. The Pareto diagram below is the result of the study.

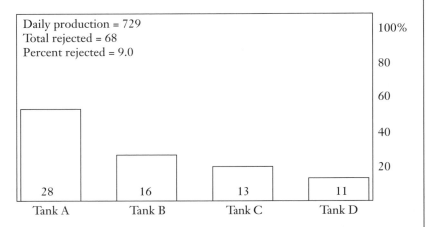

Based on the above analysis, which tank should be monitored? Tank A certainly appears to be the culprit; however, assuming that something is indeed wrong with tank A and that a corrective action is implemented (see paragraph 4.14), the corrective action should be monitored to ensure that a similar problem does not recur. In other words, tank A might only represent the apparent cause; the problem may well be related to a yet undiscovered cause. Hence the need to monitor corrective action.

Figure 15.1. An example of a Pareto diagram.

Note

1. F. Gryna, "Quality Improvements," section 22 in *Quality Control Handbook*, 3d ed., by J. M. Juran and F. M. Gryna Jr. (New York: McGraw- Hill, 1974), 22.19.

16   Histograms

Potential ISO 9001 Application:
Most Paragraphs

Histograms provide a pictorial representation of variability in a set of numbers. Without the help of a personal computer, histograms can be a bit tedious but not difficult to produce. With the help of statistical software, histograms are produced in seconds. Histograms are only effective if at least 25–30 numbers are collected. For less than 30 observations, other techniques are available. The idea behind the concept of a histogram is to classify data into groups. The number of groupings is determined by the number of observations. The interval between each grouping is determined by the range between the largest and smallest number. For example, suppose that the result of some investigation resulted in the collection of the following 25 measurements.

$$55, 64, 62, 52, 50,$$
$$55, 49, 32, 36, 32,$$
$$63, 60, 73, 53, 50,$$
$$56, 54, 28, 50, 44,$$
$$55, 54, 57, 41, 53$$

How would you group these numbers, and into how many categories? Although some formulas have been proposed by mathematicians, there are no precise ways to answer this question. Most statisticians would suggest that you should have at least 3–5 observations per category, but that is not always possible.

Suppose we decided to regroup the data into five categories. What should be the range or interval for each category?

Compute the range of the data—the difference between the largest (maximum) number and the smallest (minimum) number. For our data, the maximum is 73 and the minimum is 28. The range is therefore

$$73 - 28 = 45$$

Since we need five categories the *interval* for each category will simply be

$$45/ 5 = 9$$

Begin with the smallest number (28) and keep adding 9 to obtain the five *intervals*. For the above data this would be as follows.

		Numbers within interval	
First interval (1)	= 28–37	4	****
Second interval (2)	= 38–47	2	**
Third interval (3)	= 48–57	14	**************
Fourth interval (4)	= 58–67	4	****
Fifth interval (5)	= 68–73	1	*

The histogram, represented by the *, is sometimes rotated 90 degrees to the left (counterclockwise).

The histogram reproduced in Figure 16.1 was generated with a statistical software package and represents a regrouping into 10 intervals of the 100 copper concentration data found in Table 16.1. The advantage of computer software is that one can quickly examine the shape of several histograms by simply asking the software to adjust the number of intervals. The normal curve drawn over the histogram helps visualize the extent of so-called normality (in the statistical sense of the word) found in the data. More sophisticated tests are available to test for normality; the graph only allows for a quick refer-

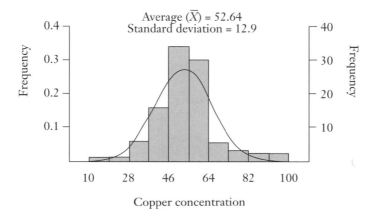

Figure 16.1. Histogram for 100 copper concentration readings.

ence. Normality testing is valuable (but not required) if one wants to perform further analysis, such as SPC, for example.

In the histogram in Figure 16.1, 52.64 represents the average of all 100 numbers. The standard deviation (12.9) is a measure of the variation found in the data. The larger the standard deviation (relative to the mean), the more variation in the data. If all 100 copper concentration readings had been exactly the same, let us say 65, for example, there would have been no variation in the data, the standard deviation would have been zero, and the histogram would have consisted of only one bar containing all 100 observations.

Compare the standard deviation computed for all 100 numbers (std. dev. = 12.9) with the *estimated* standard deviation computed on page 190 of the SPC section. Figure 16.2 combines the histogram with a plot of the 100 observations (20 samples each consisting of five readings). Both graphs represent the same data but differently. The histogram groups the 100 observations into 10 categories and helps the reader visualize the amount of variation in the data. The plot (to the right of the histogram) presents the same observations through time. Together, the two graphs represent the essential elements of SPC.

Table 16.1. Copper concentration and number of defective boards for tank A. (Five random samples per hour)

Hour	Defect	Sample 1	Sample 2	Sample 3	Sample 4	Sample 5	Mean	Range	St. dev.
7:30–7:59	0	55	64	62	52	50	56.6	14	6.15
8:00–8:29	3	55	49	32	36	32	40.8	23	10.56
8:30–8:59	0	63	60	73	53	50	59.8	23	9.03
9:00–9:29	1	56	54	28	50	44	46.4	28	11.26
9:30–9:59	1	55	54	57	41	53	52.0	16	6.32
10:00–10:29	0	38	49	51	48	30	43.2	21	8.92
10:30–10:59	2	53	64	70	42	50	55.8	28	11.18
11:00–11:29	2	40	56	44	53	43	47.2	16	6.9
11:30–11:59	0	85	60	46	46	49	57.2	39	14.8
12:30–12:59	0	50	54	57	61	69	58.2	19	7.26
13:00–13:29	0	93	52	59	75	97	75.2	45	19.95
13:30–13:59	2	60	46	59	48	50	52.6	14	6.46
7:30–7:59	1	43	63	55	38	55	50.8	25	10.10
8:00–8:29	0	53	37	46	82	55	54.6	45	16.86
8:30–8:59	0	54	21	54	41	45	43.0	33	13.54
9:00–9:29	1	37	39	57	75	49	51.4	38	15.45
9:30–9:59	0	62	50	51	57	43	52.6	19	7.23
10:00–10:29	0	48	57	56	59	63	56.6	15	5.5
10:30–10:59	3	59	16	64	45	49	46.6	48	18.7
11:00–11:29	0	32	47	60	63	60	52.4	31	12.9

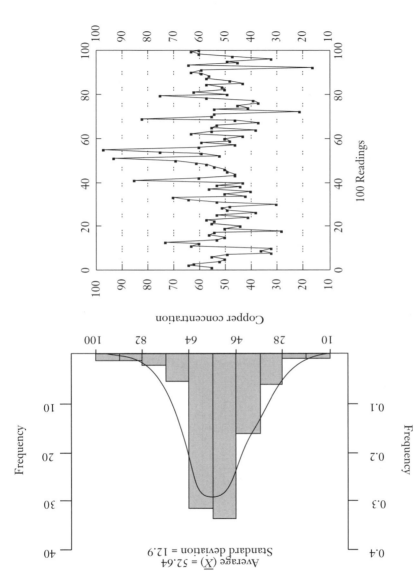

Figure 16.2. Histogram and associated plot.

17   Statistical Process Control

Potential ISO 9001 Application: Paragraphs 4.9, 4.10, 4.11, 4.14, and 4.20

SPC is the application of statistical techniques for measuring and analyzing the variation in a process. There are two basic types of control charts: variable and attribute charts. Variable charts are used when measurements such as temperature, pressure, dimensions, flow rates, weight, and so forth can be obtained by using an instrument. In attribute charts, the data consist of simple counts of number defectives or number of defective items. Examples would include number of scratches per unit or per 10 units, number of defective shipments, number of typing errors per page, number of defective parts per batch, and so on. The most common variable charts are known as X-bar and range $(\overline{X}\text{--}R)$ charts. The most common types of attribute charts are p charts, for fraction defective, and c charts, for number of defects per unit.

The level of mathematics needed to prepare $\overline{X}\text{--}R$ charts only requires the ability to compute averages and ranges, which are then plotted on graphs known as control or Shewhart charts. Although the mathematical computations are rather simple, the statistical theory behind SPC is less than trivial, but not necessarily difficult to grasp.

Some of the fundamental principals of SPC include: process stability and process capability.

A process is said to be statistically stable if it represents the same population of observations. This may not mean much to most non-statistically minded individuals. A process is said to be stable if its performance, measured by some characteristic, does not change significantly over time. An analogy might be helpful. If you were to measure and chart the average daily temperature on a tropical island, you would see very little variation or oscillation from day to day, week to week, and month to month. The tropical weather process could be said to be stable. Given the stability and thus predictability of the process, you could predict the temperature for the next day or week with great accuracy. Once in a while, some special conditions (causes), such as tropical storms, would cause the temperature to fluctuate beyond normal ranges and become temporarily unstable. But in the long run, the climate would be undisturbed, and the special conditions would be recorded on our graph as special (assignable) causes. A similar explanation could be made for industrial or administrative processes.

Within the industrial and administrative world, customers often set specifications and sometimes tolerances within which a process is expected to operate. Consequently, in the industrial world, it is not sufficient for a process to be stable; it must also be capable of satisfying customer requirements (which sometimes can be unreasonable due to reasons beyond the scope of this book). A process is said to be statistically capable if it operates within certain well-defined statistical limits known as upper and lower control limits. The difference or range between the upper and lower control limit must in turn be a fraction of the tolerance range. If these conditions are satisfied, the process is said to be capable. As a statistical technique, SPC is naturally suited to help you anticipate potential problems in your processes (for example, observing process shifts) and thus prevent their occurrence (see 4.14.3) by correcting or adjusting process parameters before it is too late.

Most control charts consist of several samples (usually 20), each consisting of five units. Naturally, the sample size can be larger or smaller, but five tends to be the optimum sample size. If you should use a smaller sample size, say two or three, *do not forget* to use different A_2, D_3, D_4, c_2 coefficients (see Table 17.1).

Figure 17.1 illustrates the basic elements of SPC. Readers interested in more information about SPC are referred to the books listed in the introduction to Part II. The data are obtained from Table 16.1 found in the histogram section. Figure 17.1 is a modification of the graph found in the histogram section. The only difference between the two graphs is that instead of plotting the 100 individual observations, Figure 17.1 plots the 20 samples, each consisting of five measurements. The resulting 20 rectangular boxes found in Figure 17.1 allow the analyst to visualize the variations not only throughout the 20 samples, but also within each sample. The longer the rectangular box, the greater the variation (or range) within a particular sample. Based on the data, with the exception of a special or assignable cause (see sample 11) yet to be explained, the process appears stable.

Assuming that the process is stable, in order to determine if the process is capable, one needs to know the specification for copper

Table 17.1. Factors for constructing variables control charts.

Observations in sample (n)	Chart for averages factors for control limits	Factor for central line	Chart for ranges	
	A_2	d_2	D_3	D_4
2	1.880	1.128	0	3.267
3	1.023	1.693	0	2.574
4	0.729	2.059	0	2.282
5	0.577	2.326	0	2.114
6	0.483	2.534	0	2.114

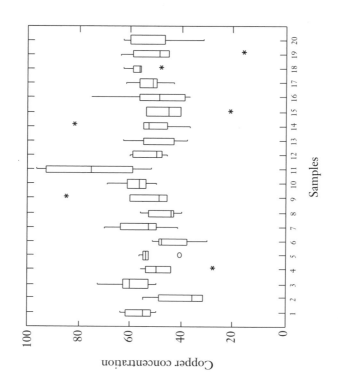

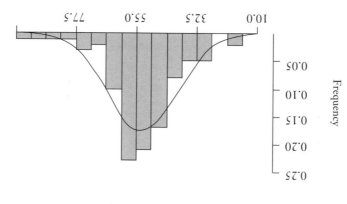

Figure 17.1. Example of $\bar{X}$–R chart with histogram.

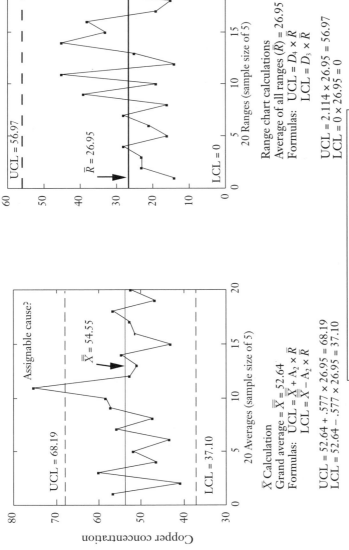

Figure 17.1. *(continued)*

concentration. Let us assume that the specifications for copper concentration are: 70 units $\pm$ 30 units (or 40 to 100).

The following computations are required to determine whether tank A is a (statistically) capable process.

1. Determine the sample size (n), which is the size of each sample taken every half an hour. For our example, $n = 5$.

2. From Table 17.1 locate the d_2 factor (2.326).

3. Compute the estimated standard deviation (denoted by the Greek letter sigma, σ) of the process using the following formula.

$$\text{Estimated standard deviation } (\sigma) = \frac{\bar{R}}{d_2}$$

For this example we have estimated standard deviation $= \dfrac{26.95}{2.326} = 11.58$

(Note: Compare this estimate with the standard deviation for the 100 values shown in the histogram found in Figure 16.2.)

4. Compute the process capability ratio (PCR) using the following formula,

$$\text{PCR} = \frac{\text{USL} - \text{LSL}}{6 \times \sigma} \text{ or PCR} = \frac{100 - 40}{6 \times 11.58} \text{ or PCR} = \frac{60}{69.51} = 0.863$$

where USL = upper specification limit and LSL = lower specification limit.

If the process runs at nominal value, the process is considered statistically capable if and only if the PCR ratio is greater than 1.0. In this example the process is nearly capable since the PCR ratio is less than 1.0. Notice, however, that the nominal value; the mid-point between the upper and lower specification, is 70.0. The process mean, the grand average $\bar{\bar{X}}$, is only 52.64. In other words, the process is running below nominal value; it is said to be off-center. If the process average could be brought up by 17 units, the process may be capable. The process is actually less capable than first assumed. Indeed, for off-centered processes the following computations apply.

$$PCR_k = \frac{mean - LSL}{3 \times \sigma} = \frac{53 - 40}{3 \times 11.58} = 0.37$$

$$PCR_k = \frac{USL - mean}{3 \times 11.58} = \frac{100 - 53}{34.74} = 1.35$$

By selecting the minimum of the two PCR_k (0.37, 1.35), one sees that the process is not capable at the low end of the specification. Centering the process will help significantly.

These statistical analyses could be used to satisfy the requirements specified in paragraph 4.20. Naturally, not all processes can be analyzed using SPC. If your processes consist of running only two units of production per month, it will take you a very long time to obtain the required data necessary to produce $\overline{X}$–R charts. Indeed the typical $\overline{X}$–R charts consist of 100 data points collected in 20 samples of five measurements each. At a production rate of two units per month, you will need 50 months to obtain the required data.

Note

1. In Brazil and other countries, median and range (median range or average range depending on preference) charts are more popular. The advantage of the median chart is that the average does not have to be computed. The median is the middle number in a series of numbers arranged according to magnitude. Mathematically, the median is the $(n + 1)/2$ number in an ordered list of numbers. For example, suppose you took five measurements and obtained the following results: 22, 18, 24, 17, 23. Rearrange the numbers from lowest to largest: 17, 18, 22, 23, 24. The median is 22, the third number. If we had four numbers, the median would be the 2.5 number or a value between the second and third number. Median and range charts use different coefficients (A_5 for the median and D_5 and D_6 for the median range.

18   Other Techniques: ANOVA and DoE

Potential ISO 9001 Application: Paragraphs 4.13, 4.14, and 4.20

As its name implies, analysis of variance (ANOVA) allows for the decomposition of the overall variance of a variable into its subcomponents. Gauge R&R studies are analyses of variance. In this case the total variation of the measurement process is hypothesized to be attributable to several components (or factors): variation between operators, variation between repeated measurements (by each operator), variation among parts, and unknown other sources collectively known as error. One could analyze the within-operator variability, the between-operator variability, and other sources of variability. The essence of ANOVA is to compare ratios of variability. These ratios, known as F tests, allow a statistician to determine whether or not component(s) or factor(s) (for example, operator, shift, supplier, type of material, method) or combinations (also known as interactions) of factors play a statistically significant role in influencing the performance of a response factor or variable, also referred to as the dependent variable.

Design of experiments (DoE) is a form of analysis of variance whereby an experimenter can control the level of certain factors and observe which, if any, of these factors or interaction of factors, would affect the overall performance of a response variable. For example, one could hypothesize that the surface roughness of an aluminum ingot is potentially influenced by a few factors such as drop speed, water rate, and thickness of the gas water interface. One could then plan an experiment in which each of these three factors would be varied and observe the effect on surface roughness. With three factors set at two levels each, one would only need to run eight experiments (or 2^3) to find out the answer to our question.

Example. Soon after a new process was installed, the process engineer noticed that the yield on product A was subject to great variability. Although the process was in statistical control, improving the yield would improve the profit margin. The company decided to investigate the problem, and a problem-solving team was assigned to the task.

The team consisting of the process engineer and operators decided to investigate the effect of three factors on product yield: temperature, concentration, and type of catalyst. Current temperature and concentration specifications called for a setting of 170° Celsius ± 5° and a concentration of 30 percent ± 5 percent. The favored catalyst was catalyst A. The process engineer decided to run a designed experiment by running the process at the following settings.

Temperature: 160 (–) degrees and 180 (+) degrees

Concentration: 20% (–) and 40% (+)

Catalysts: A (–) and B (+)

Since three factors will be controlled and each factor will be set at two settings, a total of eight runs are required to run what is known as a full factorial design. Table 18.1 shows the experimental runs and the resulting yield in product for each combination of settings. For ease of computation, the settings have been recorded as + and –. (Note: The matrix of + and – is known as an orthogonal matrix.)

The numbers in the estimate column are computed by moving down a factor column and adding or subtracting the yield (y). The average is the average of all eight yields. For example, the value of 23.0 associated with factor T is computed as follows:

1. Reading down the T column, the signs read as follows: −, +, −, +, −, +, −, and +.

2. Multiplying the yield value (y) with the appropriate sign and adding down the column we obtain

$$- 60 + 72 - 54 + 68 - 52 + 83 - 45 + 80 = 92 \div 4 = 23$$

We divide by 4 because there are four pluses and four minuses. The division by 8 is used for the computation of the grand average. The estimated effect for temperature is therefore 23. This means that an increase in temperature can increase yield by as much as 23 grams. Can you verify this by looking at the data? Similarly, you can see that a decrease in concentration can actually reduce yield by 5.0 grams. This is a significant finding because it indicates that rather than running at the current 30 percent setting, concentration could be reduced to 20 percent thus saving some money. Finally, an increase of 10 grams can be generated by the right combination or interaction of temperature and catalyst (TK). Can you tell which combination is best?

3. Similar computations are performed for the estimated effect for concentration (C); the concentration $\times$ temperature interaction effect (TC); the catalyst effect (K); the temperature $\times$ catalyst interaction (TK); the concentration $\times$ catalyst interaction effect (CK); and the temperature $\times$ concentration $\times$ catalyst effect (TCK).

But how do we know which effect is significant, that is, more important than the others? It would appear that temperature (T) with a value of +23.0, concentration (C) with a value of −5.0, and temperature and catalyst (TK) with a value of +10.0 are more important than the others, but how can the information be quantified? There are several techniques available but one easy technique to use is the log-normal probability plot. Table 18.2 illustrates the steps.

Computations for P for $i = 1, 2,$ and 7 are as follows:

For $i = 1$, $P = 100 (1-0.5)/7 = 100 (0.5)/7 = 50/7 = 7.14$

For $i = 2$, $P = 100 (2-0.5)/7 = 100 (1.5)/7 = 150/7 = 21.42$

For $i = 7$, $P = 100 (7-0.5)/7 = 100 (6.5)/7 = 650/7 = 92.85$

The percentage values (P) are next plotted on semilogarithmic graph paper (that is, the vertical Y-axis is based on the logarithmic scale).

Table 18.1. Design of experiment computations.

Run number	Temperature (°C) T	Concentration (%) C	Catalyst (A or B) K	Yield (grams) y	Estimate	Factor
1	160	20	A	60	64.25	average
2	180	20	A	72	23.0	T
3	160	40	A	54	−5.0	C
4	180	40	A	68	1.5	TC
5	160	20	B	52	1.5	K
6	180	20	B	83	10.0	TK
7	160	40	B	45	0.0	CK
8	180	40	B	80	0.5	TCK

Coded factors			Divisor	y
−	−	−	8	60
+	−	−	4	72
−	+	−	4	54
+	+	−	4	68
−	−	+	4	52
+	−	+	4	83
−	+	+	4	45
+	+	+	4	80

Source: Box, George E. P., Hunter, William G., and Hunter, J. Stuart. *Statistics for Experimenters: An Introduction to Design, Data Analysis, and Model Building.* © John Wiley & Sons, Inc., 1978. Reprinted with permission of John Wiley & Sons, Inc., p. 308.

Table 18.2. Probability points for log-normal plot.

Order number i	1	2	3	4	5	6	7
Effect	−5.0	0.0	0.5	1.5	1.5	10	23
Identity of effects	3	7	8	4	5	6	2
P(%) = 100 (i - 0.5)/7 7 = number of runs −1	7.14	21.42	35.71	50.0	64.28	78.57	92.85

Source: Box, George E. P., Hunter, William G., and Hunter, J. Stuart. *Statistics for Experimenters: An Introduction to Design, Data Analysis, and Model Building.* © John Wiley & Sons, Inc., 1978. Reprinted with permisission of John Wiley & Sons, Inc., adapted from p. 332.

The results are shown in Figure 18.1. Points that fall outside the straight line indicate significant factors, factors that are likely to have a statistical significant impact on the yield. These points are point 3 (concentration effect), point 6 (temperature × catalyst interaction), and point 2 (temperature).

The experiment demonstrates that the yield can be improved by increasing the temperature, reducing the concentration, and using catalyst B.

ANOVAs and DoEs are very powerful and efficient statistical techniques that can be used in any application that requires process optimization. The techniques can also be used to quantitatively verify whether or not a corrective action has been effective. The advantages of these techniques remain to be fully explored by all industries within the manufacturing and service sectors.

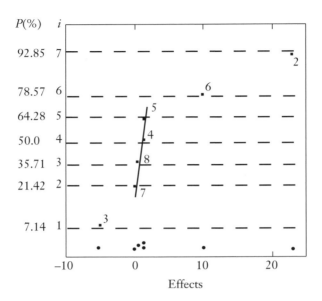

Figure 18.1. Normal plot for yield experiment.

Source: Box, George E. P., Hunter, William G., and Hunter, J. Stuart. *Statistics for Experimenters: An Introduction to Design, Data Analysis, and Model Building.* © John Wiley & Sons, Inc., 1978. Reprinted with permisission of John Wiley & Sons, Inc., adapted from p. 331.

19　Conclusions

The implementation of an ISO 9000 quality assurance system need not be onerous. As stated in the Preface, implementation costs tend to rapidly get out of control for basically one reason: the quality assurance system is too complicated and detailed. Developing a complex system is not as difficult as maintaining it, so always try to develop as simple a system as possible. Do not try to be too clever when writing a document control procedure, for example. Avoid the need for multiple signatures, and, if at all possible, rely on computers to document and maintain your system. Maintaining a quality assurance system can be a rather tedious and thankless task, so rely on technology to facilitate your job.

Ever since the ISO 9000 phenomenon began to spread around the world, businesses over the globe began to develop elaborate quality assurance systems. Procedures were written for just about every function or activity. Over the past six years I have seen procedures on how to answer a phone, procedures on how to fill out a form, even procedures on procedures. The number of procedures written ever since the ISO 9000 standards were published in 1987 must be enormous. Assume that each organization ends up writing, on average, 50 procedures (a conservative estimate), and assume further that approximately 80,000 sites were registered to one of the ISO 9000 standards as of mid-1995. Based on these conservative figures we can estimate that approximately 4,000,000 procedures have already been written from Ankara to Zagreb. An impressive number of pages indeed! Pity the poor auditors who must read these procedures. My purpose with this book has been to suggest that a quality assurance system need not be elaborate in order to be effective. I trust I have convinced you. If there are only three things you remember from this book, I hope they are these.

Document what is required, but only as much as you need to improve your overall quality, efficiency, and productivity.

Avoid documenting what should be covered under training.

Always test and verify the validity of your system, and do not hesitate to simplify or otherwise improve it as often as possible.

Appendix
Review of ISO 9003 Requirements

Comparing the ISO 9003 standard with ISO 9001 or ISO 9002, one notices that the words "shall establish and maintain documented procedures" are not included in every paragraph. Consequently, ISO 9003 allows for greater flexibility in interpretation and is much less burdensome on documentation requirements. The only significant differences between ISO 9003 and the other standards are as follows.

4.1.2.1 Responsibility and Authority
This paragraph is significantly shorter. One only needs to define the responsibility and authority of persons who "conduct final inspection and tests" and "ensure that finished product that does not conform to specified requirements is prevented from being used or delivered."[1]

4.2.3 Quality Planning
Since ISO 9003 does not include design control, there are only seven (instead of eight in ISO 9001 and ISO 9002) subclauses. The subclauses are slightly rephrased to reflect the ISO 9003 emphasis on final inspection. For example, in ISO 9001, paragraph 4.2.3a has the words "the preparation of quality plans;" the same paragraph in ISO 9003 reads "the preparation of quality plans for final inspection and tests."

4.4 Design Control
This section is not applicable.

4.6 Purchasing
This section is not applicable.

4.8 Product Identification and Traceability
The paragraph is simplified to reflect the fact that ISO 9003 organizations do not produce, deliver, or install products.

4.9 Process Control
This section is not applicable.

4.10 Inspection and Testing
This paragraph only consists of two subparagraphs *(General* and *Final Inspection and Testing)* instead of the five found in ISO 9001 and ISO 9002. Final Inspection and Testing section is more condensed to reflect the limitations of ISO 9003.

4.13 Control of Nonconforming Product
The paragraph is a combination of 4.13.1 and 4.13.2 found in ISO 9001 and ISO 9002. It reads as follows:

> The supplier shall establish and maintain control of product that does not conform to specified requirements to ensure that unintended use or delivery is avoided.

> Control shall provide for identification, documentation, evaluation, segregation (when practical), disposition of nonconforming product and for notification to the functions concerned.

> The description of repairs, and of any nonconformity that has been accepted under authorized concession, shall be recorded to denote the actual condition. (See 4.16).

> Repaired and/or reworked product shall be re-inspected in accordance with the quality plan and/or documented procedure requirements.

4.14 Corrective Action

As with paragraph 4.13, this paragraph is also substantially reduced. The requirements follow.

The supplier shall:

> a) investigate nonconformities that have been identified from the analysis of final inspection and test reports and customer complaints of product;
>
> b) determine and implement appropriate corrective action on the nonconformities;
>
> c) ensure that relevant information on the actions taken is submitted for management review (see 4.1.3).

4.16 Control of Quality Records

This section is rephrased from ISO 9001, but notably no requirement for a documented procedure is mentioned. Also, the requirement to identify, collect, index, access, file, store, and dispose of records is taken out, thus reducing the length of the text. The need to maintain records on subcontractors is also left out, which is logical because ISO 9003–type companies do not manufacture a product, but they could subcontract a service.

4.19 Servicing

This section is not applicable.

4.20 Statistical Techniques

The Procedures paragraph is left out. The clause simply states that "The supplier shall identify the need for statistical techniques required for the acceptability of product characteristic" and implement and control their application. All other paragraphs are essentially the same.

Note

1. All quoted material in this appendix is from ISO 9003, unless otherwise stated.

Index